STARS&CARS

MYTHICAL PAIRINGS

Quarto is the authority on a wide range of topics.
Quarto educates, entertains and enriches the lives of our readers –
enthusiasts and lovers of hands-on living
www.QuartoKnows.com

Editors : Sara Quemener et Mathilde Boisserie
Picture research : Jeanne Daucé et Mathilde Boisserie
Creative director : Philippe Marchand
Art director : Émilie Greenberg
Layout design : Marion Alfano
Illustrations : Thomas Hamel
Text editing : Sandrine Harbonnier et Catherine Decayeux
Repro : Cédric Delsart
Production : Stéphanie Parlange

Translation : Paul Carslake

Conceived by Copyright Éditions
104, boulevard Arago
75014 Paris – France
© 2016, 2017 Copyright Éditions, Paris

First published in Great Britain
2017 by Aurum Press Ltd
74–77 White Lion Street
Islington
London N1 9PF

A catalogue record for this book is available from the British Library.

ISBN 978 1 78131 676 4
eISBN 978 1 78131 697 9

10 9 8 7 6 5 4 3 2 1
2021 2020 2019 2018 2017

Printed in Czech Republic

JACQUES BRAUNSTEIN

STARS&CARS
MYTHICAL PAIRINGS

Aurum
Press

DRIVING
LEGENDS

The invention of the car and the birth of cinema took place within just five years of each other. Gottlieb Daimler built his petrol-powered quadricycle in 1886 (the first of what we know today as Mercedes cars). Meanwhile, on the other side of the Atlantic, Thomas Edison began showing film projections in 1891. Notably, one of the first films to draw in the crowds was the Lumière brothers' *The Arrival of A Train In The Station at La Ciotat* (1886). During the film, the steam locomotive appeared to come crashing into the movie theatre at full speed – and the spectators were completely terrified. And so the action movie was born, and before long car chases became a recurring theme in the movies. From the very beginning of the 20th century, actors such as Harold Lloyd or Buster Keaton created comic storylines involving cars – and especially the Model T Ford – the first car to be built on a production line (in 1908).

At the same time, cinema's relationship with celebrity changed. Previously, people could see actors, singers and other performers live, on stage. With the advent of cinema, movie stars became more distant and mysterious – while their popularity became international. Newspapers and magazines were feeding an insatiable public demand for news, pictures and gossip about their favourite stars. And the celebrities themselves, suddenly immensely wealthy, began to adopt the way of life of the European aristocracy – building palatial homes in the Hollywood hills, dressing in bespoke suits and couture fashion – and buying the most fashionable new cars.

Italian-born Rudolph Valentino, the star of *The Sheik* (1921), bought (from Europe) and shipped (at enormous expense) such iconic brands as Rolls Royce, Avions Voisin and Isotta Fraschini. Another A-list celebrity of the time, Mary Pickford, the star of *Daddy-Long-Legs* (1919), also displayed a passion for cars – and drove them herself, favouring the Delage, Rolls Royce, and an early Ford Model A in 1928.

Jean Harlow (Cadillac) and Rita Hayworth (Lincoln) followed suit. The car was an indication of a new level of independence for these women: they led their lives and drove their careers in exactly the same way: with their foot firmly to the floor. As a symbol of both modernity and speed, the automobile was a winner. Everybody dreamed of owning one. And those who could own one dreamed of owning cars even more expensive, powerful and luxurious.

Businessmen, artists, royals, the rich and super-rich all became drawn into an increasingly competitive game of owning the fastest, the newest, the most beautiful car. Automobile design became a kind of couture fashion, with top designers building extraordinarily beautiful bespoke automobiles which they would show off to the world in jaw-dropping exhibitions.

So the world would see Gary Cooper in a Duesenberg or a Cadillac V16, Clark Gable in a Packard, and Errol Flynn driving an Auburn. Writers and novelists who could afford to, joined in: Francis Scott Fitzgerald bought himself a Rolls, Paul Morand a Bugatti. You could not be a real star without the car.

All this seems a long way from where we are today. The image of the car for many people – including film stars - has become linked with environmental pollution. Even so, there are still plenty of sports stars, as well as big names in the music business, who are ready to step into some amazing cars. Take world champion boxer Floyd Mayweather Jr, for example, with his two Rolls Royces and three Bugattis. Or Jay Z and Kanye West who, in the *Otis* video, take a chainsaw to cut through a Maybach (the most exclusive Mercedes brand on the planet) to create their very own custom-built vehicle in the spirit of Mad Max: a game to be played only by the very, very rich.

And stars are still prepared to pay top dollar for the real classics. At the start of 2016, Lionel Messi and Cristiano Ronaldo, the elite of the Spanish soccer league, were reportedly bidding against each other for a 1957 Ferrari 335 S, which was eventually sold for 32 million euros at Paris auction house Artcurial (Messi won the bid). This exceptional auction price points to the existence of a kind of golden age of car design from the late 1950s to the early 1960s. Within a period of just five years, an incredible range of iconic models came to life: the Ferrari 250 California, the E-Type Jaguar, the Porsche 911, the Aston Martin DB 5, the Ford Mustang. Paradoxically, this was also the *end* of the golden Hollywood era, and movie stars during the 1960s were more independent-minded than their predecessors. You would not find Steve McQueen, in stark contrast to Gable or Cooper, sitting at the wheel grinning for the camera, and many of the pictures from this era are infused with a sense of rather downbeat reality. By the mid-1960s, stars of pop and rock had become the new A-listers, and were challenging everything. The Beatles and the Rolling Stones rejected the old order but still posed for photos, with long hair and flared jeans, alongside their Aston Martins and Ferraris. The oil price rises in the 1970s, the introduction of more and more speed limits on the roads, and a growing uniformity in car production across the world saw this period come to a close. And despite a resurgence in the 1980s (*Magnum*, *Miami Vice*, *Risky Business* ...) the marriage of film stars and the cars they drove became more about nostalgia: think about the 1966 Ford Thunderbird in *Thelma and Louise*, or Ryan Gosling's 1973 Chevrolet Chevelle in *Drive*. In this book, then, we have chosen to focus essentially on the cars from this golden age of the 1950s to the 1980s, with their impeccable style and beautiful bodywork, and on the stars – the actors, writers, artists and musicians – who drove them.

ACTORS WHO

STEVE MCQUEEN **FORD MUSTANG GT FASTBACK 1968**

JAMES DEAN **& HIS PORSCHES**

PAUL NEWMAN **PORSCHE 911 S 1969**

AND THE REST **ACTORS AND RACERS**

RACE

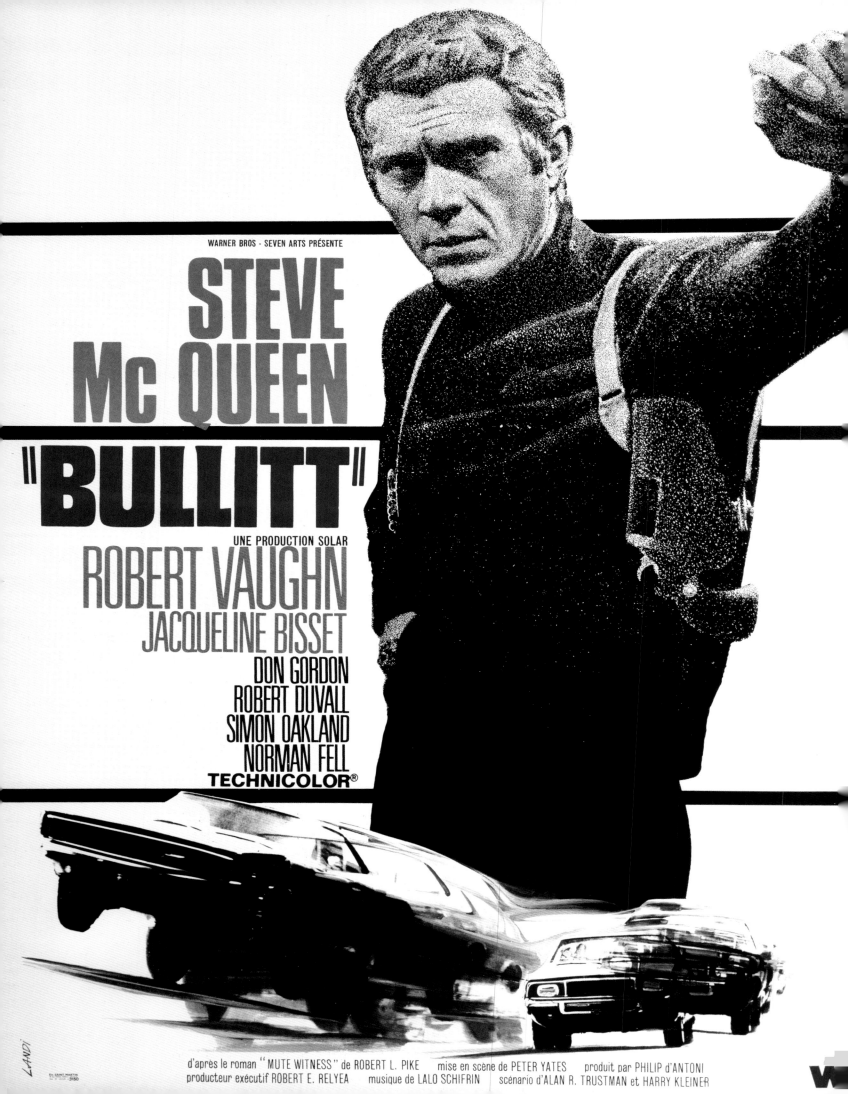

STEVE MCQUEEN
& FORD MUSTANG
GT FASTBACK 1968

> 'I'M NOT SURE WHETHER
> I'M AN ACTOR WHO RACES
> OR A RACER WHO ACTS'
>
> STEVE MCQUEEN

For film fans and car enthusiasts alike, Steve McQueen represents the ultimate combination of actor and racing driver. In the film *Bullitt* in 1968, he took part in the most famous car chase in the history of cinema. And three years later, in *Le Mans* (1971) he starred in – and produced – what has come to be known as the most realistic film ever made on motor racing.

For McQueen, a passion for machines ran through his blood. As a boy on his grandfather's farm, he used to help fix the tractors and during his military service, he tuned up the engine of his battle tank. In 1950, when he went to New York to study acting, he bought a motorcycle sidecar that he repaired and restored himself, whilst also finding the time to fix up the motorbikes of his Actors Studio colleagues, including James Dean.

He bought his first sports car in 1952, at the age of 22. It was British: an MG TC, which he bought partly with money made on Broadway, and partly with winnings from playing poker. A few years later, when he became the star of the TV series *In The Name Of The Law* (1958-1961), he was finally able to buy a brand new car: a black 1958 Porsche 356 1600 Speedster – the same model, incidentally, that both James Dean

and Paul Newman happened to own. McQueen however, set to work tuning up the engine for additional power, fitting rapid release wheels and anti-roll bars, and took it to the track. Eighteen months, and three race-wins later, he sold the 356 for the even more powerful Lotus Eleven. And after the Lotus, he chose a Jaguar XK-SS, a rare racing roadster with characteristically sinuous bodywork. But the film studio's insurers insisted that he give up motor racing. He had no choice but to comply, and instead started an automotive collection, buying several dozen cars, more than one hundred motorcycles and several aircraft.

McQueen's collection was exceptional, (and part of it can be seen in a parking garage scene towards the beginning of *Bullitt*). It included the elegant 1964 Ferrari 250 Lusso which he gave to his wife Neile for her 34th birthday; and a Porsche 911 in slate grey with a manual five-speed gearbox – identical to the car which appears at the very start of the film *Le Mans*. In fact he preferred his own manual gearbox 911 to the Sportmatic version that Porsche had given him for the film, complaining that the electric windows made the car heavier and slower.

Dune Buggy
For *The Thomas Crown Affair* (1968), Steve McQueen ordered a specially made Manx Dune Buggy with an eye-wateringly powerful 230 bhp engine for a race scene on the beach. Faye Dunaway was in the passenger seat.

His collection also included a Mercedes 300 SEL 6.3l – a powerful saloon car that he first discovered when one shot past him on a German autobahn while McQueen himself was driving at 130mph (200km/h) in a Porsche. After that, he just had to have one.

McQueen had a habit of systematically modifying most of the cars he owned in some way, either mechanically (he bought a Jeep into which he swapped in a Chevrolet V8 engine) or aesthetically (he bought a Ferrari 275 GTS/4 and sent it off for a re-spray the day it was delivered). The Mercedes was in fact the same as that driven by Faye Dunaway, his co-star in *The Thomas Crown Affair*, (and it subsequently got into an accident just after leaving the garage).

Meanwhile, the actor was also getting into motocross, thanks to a Triumph motorcycle dealer in Los Angeles called Bud Ekins. Ekins was a stunt double for McQueen both for the bike sequence in *The Great Escape*, and also for some of the most demanding precision stunts of the iconic pursuit sequence in *Bullitt* through the streets of San Francisco in 1968. That ten-minute scene became a defining moment in the cinematic car chase, and went on to be copied and adapted in innumerable films, such as *The French Connection* and *The Burglars* (both 1971).

Steve McQueen with the
1965 Lola T70, in which he
took part in endurance racing
in the USA before switching
to the Porsche 908, which
gave him a second place in
the Twelve Hours of Sebring
endurance race in 1970.

Le Mans

Between filming, McQueen took part in dirt track
bike racing as often as he could, mainly in the
desert around Los Angeles. The documentary film
On Any Sunday, which he produced in 1971, has
since become the classic for fans of custom bikes.
In the film, McQueen is on a 'Husky' Husqvarna
400, and delivers one of the best quotes: 'Every
time I start thinking the world is all bad, then I
start seeing people out there having a good time
on motorcycles. It makes me take another look.' A
decade earlier in England, while filming *The War
Lover* in 1962, he had once signed up (under a
false name) to race at the Brands Hatch circuit
(and met champion driver Stirling Moss).

McQueen really wanted to combine his twin
passions – as actor and driver – and in 1971 he
succeeded with what was to become the definitive
motor racing movie: *Le Mans*. McQueen came up
with an idea for making special camera supports,
which allowed filming of high-speed action from
three cameras fitted to a Porsche 908 during the
'live' Le Mans 24 Hours race in 1970. This was to be
a game changer in terms of the ability to immerse
the film's audience in the live race action at very
close quarters.

McQueen himself was denied the chance to
drive in the film. Even though, several months
earlier, he had finished in second place in the Twelve
Hours of Sebring endurance race; in *Le Mans*, it was
once again insurance policy exclusions that meant a
disappointed McQueen was deprived of actual
driving time on the race track. For McQueen, this
was a real blow. As the character he plays in the
film, race driver Michael Delaney, puts it: 'When

you're racing, it's life. Anything that happens
before or after is just waiting.'

Filming *Le Mans* became a long and drawn-out
enterprise. Working without a fixed screenplay, for
over three months McQueen kept adding more
and more angles and shots, and switched director
along the way. Notably, one of the professional
drivers, David Piper, lost a leg in an accident during
the filming. On its launch, the film met with little
critical acclaim. Despite good enough box office
receipts, and its growing cult status among fans,
the film seemed to have shattered something
inside McQueen, who afterwards never again
raced competitively. His passion for driving did not
disappear though, and it was often during the
night, on the steep and winding hairpin bends of a
nearly empty Mulholland Drive in the Hollywood
hills, that he was still able to put some of his
performance cars through their paces.

On the dashboard of his Porsche 930 Turbo
(and on the dash of many of his other cars), he
had installed a switch that would turn off the
rear lights (but leave the headlights on) when
driving at night because, he said, he did not want
to be followed. Given the speed and skill with
which he drove his 260 bhp Porsche, that was
one unlikely scenario.

'WHEN YOU'RE RACING, IT'S LIFE.
ANYTHING THAT HAPPENS BEFORE
OR AFTER IS JUST WAITING'
STEVE MCQUEEN IN *LE MANS* (1971)

FORD
MUSTANG GT FASTBACK 1968

ENGINE
Configuration **8-cylinder, V8**
Capacity **6391 cc**
Fuel **Petrol**
Layout **Front engine, longitudinal**

TRANSMISSION
Gearbox **4-speed, manual**
Drive type **Rear wheel drive**

DIMENSIONS
Length **4.66 m** / Width **1.80 m**
Height **1.31 m**
Weight **1515 kg**

PERFORMANCE
Power **325 bhp**

① The ultimate car chase

The chase sequence in the film lasted ten minutes. Filming, however, took three weeks. The sound recording was exceptionally good, emphasising the difference between the two cars – the higher-pitched Mustang, and the more muted growl of the Dodge Charger R/T.

② Bigger and better

The new 1968 Mustangs were bigger and faster than the previous models – with the aim of keeping an edge over new rivals such as the Chevrolet Camaro and the Dodge Charger.

③ Prepped for the race

Ford Motor Company lent the two 390GT models used for the filming of *Bullitt* to Warner. The engines, brakes and suspension were modified for the film by motor racing veteran Max Balchowsky.

④ Clean lines

At the request of Steve McQueen, Carroll Shelby (the man who created the AC Cobra and the racing versions of the Mustang) personally removed the badges and chrome-work on the Mustang for *Bullitt*.

McQueen and machine
Steve McQueen with the Ferrari 312 P
driven by his opponent in the film
Le Mans (1971)

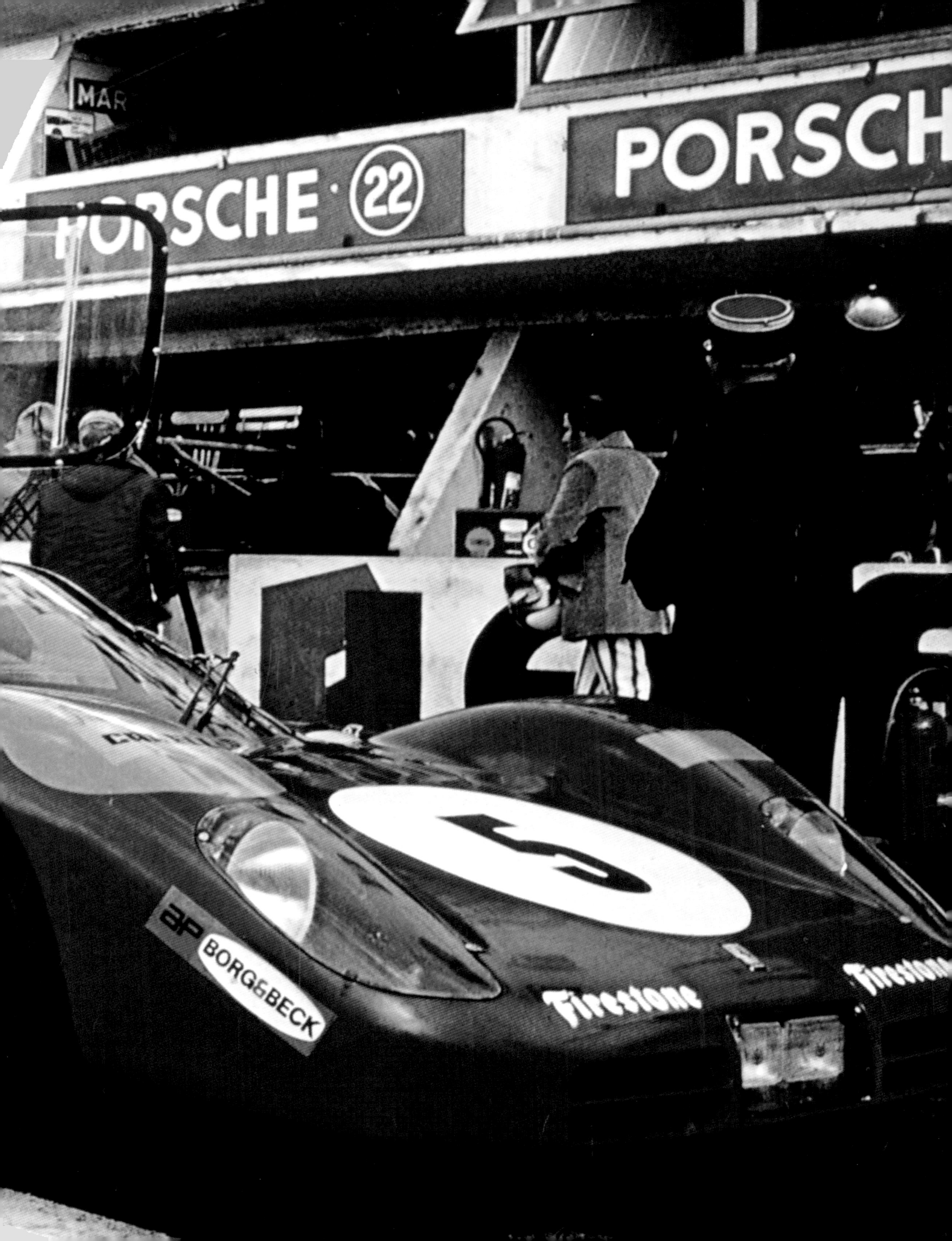
MAR
PORSCHE · 22
PORSCHE
BORG&BECK
Firestone
Firestone

'DREAM AS IF YOU'LL LIVE FOREVER.'
JAMES DEAN

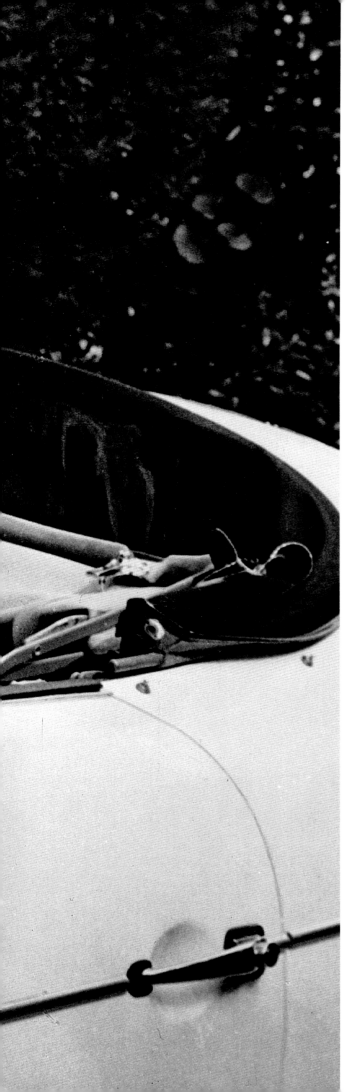

JAMES DEAN
& PORSCHE

356 SPEEDSTER (PRE-A) 1955

SPYDER 550 1955

First love
In 1955, James Dean bought his
first Porsche – a 356 Speedster
– and took it racing on local
circuits whenever he could.

On 30 September 1955, James Dean took to
the road in his Porsche Spyder 550 to
compete in a racing event at Salinas, California,
that was taking place the following day. In the
passenger seat was his mechanic, Rolf Wütherich,
and following behind them, in a white Ford estate
car, was another mechanic and a photographer.

Dean had just finished filming *Giant* and, as
usual, a clause in his contract had barred him
from taking part in motor racing or any other kind
of driving deemed to be dangerous. [Shortly
before, he had, however, taken part in a short film
about road safety, encouraging drivers to be
more careful on the road.] Now, with the filming
finished, and with just a few voice parts left to
record, he was itching to get back on the
racetrack. He knew the Salinas circuit well – it was
where he had filmed *East of Eden* which had just
been released.

The Spyder 550, bought a few weeks earlier at
the Los Angeles Porsche showroom run by John
von Neumann, was much more of an out-and-out
racecar than the Porsche 356, which Dean had
driven earlier in his career. At 5.55 p.m., after four
hours of driving (and one speeding fine), Dean's
Spyder arrived at the intersection between
Highway 446 and Highway 41. At the same
moment, Donald Turnupseed, a student driving

Rebel Without a Cause
The race scene in *Rebel Without A Cause*: impossible to watch without calling to mind Dean's impending death. The film was released one month after Dean's fatal accident, and made him an instant star.

Two legends of the road
Dean with his Porsche Spyder.

Rebel Without A Cause

Several weeks later, on 27 October 1955, *Rebel Without A Cause* was released. One scene in the film seemed especially prescient. In a feat of bravado, Dean's character Jim Stark drives his car, a 1941 Chevrolet Special Deluxe, towards a cliff edge and then jumps from the car just a few yards from the precipice. His rival in this dangerous game fails to exit his own car and plunges to his death over the cliff.

It was during the filming of *Rebel Without A Cause* that Dean got a taste for motor racing, and bought his first Porsche, a 356 Speedster 1500 Super, with which he was endlessly photographed – and in fact many people believed that it was in this car that he died. The film, which portrayed a rebellious, troubled, and fragile adolescent, instantly made James Dean the symbol of a new generation that was suffocating beneath the conservative and conformist American values of the 1950s. The car took on a new role as a symbol of this rebellion, as did the motorcycle with its symbolic role underlined by the Marlon Brando film *The Wild One* in 1953. In rock music, it made its cinematic debut in the film *Blackboard Jungle* in 1955 and some years later Elvis Presley revealed that Dean had been his own role model. And so a legend was born.

a 1950 Ford Tudor Sedan, failed to see the small roadster approaching the junction on his left side, and drove into the road, straight into its path. The Spyder slammed straight into the front section of the Ford from the side, just forward of the driver's door.

The shock of the accident threw Dean's mechanic out of the car, which saved his life. But for Dean the impact was fatal. The layout of the mid-engined Spyder meant that in front of the driver was an empty boot space: there was nothing to absorb any impact as it slammed into the side of the Ford's massive engine. Dean died on the way to hospital. The driver of the Ford Tudor escaped with minor injuries.

PORSCHE
356 SPEEDSTER
(PRE-A) 1955

ENGINE
Configuration **4-cylinder, flat-four**
Capacity **1488 cc**
Fuel **Petrol**
Layout **Rear engine, longitudinal**

TRANSMISSION
Gearbox **4-speed, manual, synchronised**
Drive type **Rear wheel drive**

DIMENSIONS
Length **4.00 m** / Width **1.60 m**
Height **1.22 m**
Weight **680 kg**

PERFORMANCE
Power **70 bhp at 5000 rpm**
Maximum speed **104 mph**

① An American special

Porsche designed this edition of the Speedster at the request of its US importer Max Hoffmann – with its low-profile V-shaped windscreen making it easier to see, and to be seen.

② Inspired by Beetle

The body shape of the 356 is in part inspired by the VW Beetle, which was also designed by Ferdinand Porsche. Its understated styling created a modern alternative to the British roadsters and Italian cabriolets, which had been a huge commercial success worldwide during the 1950s.

③ A dynasty is born

With its rear engine layout and round headlights, the 356 was pointing the way to the Porsche 911, which remains the flagship of the Porsche brand to this day.

④ Stripped for racing

Wheel trims, chrome, wing mirrors – James Dean wanted to race his 356, and stripped off what he saw as 'superfluous' styling elements.

PAUL NEWMAN
& PORSCHE

911 'S' 1969

'IT IS USELESS TO PUT ON YOUR BRAKES WHEN YOU'RE UPSIDE DOWN.'

PAUL NEWMAN

Paul Newman became a movie star in the 1950s (with movies like *The Left Handed Gun* and *Cat on a Hot Tin Roof*, both 1958). He was not fanatical about cars right from the start, though like other film stars of his time, he typically drove upscale brands like Cadillac and Porsche. All that changed in 1968, when he took on the role of an Indy Car driver in the film *Winning*. He got a taste for the race and began, at the age of 43, a motor

racing career that was to last for the rest of his life. The death of Newman's eldest son, a victim of a drug overdose, in some ways reinforced this passion for racing: Newman once observed that it was only when racing that he was able to stop thinking about his son.

Newman's high point came in 1979 when he signed on for the 24 Hours of Le Mans in a team with Rolf Stommelen and Dick Barbour, driving a Porsche 935 (the race version of the Porsche 930 Turbo). The team finished in second place, just as the car's engine was about to die. In the closing minutes of the race, Barbour waited on the finish line for the winning car to take first place, rather than run the risk of starting another 8.5-mile lap of the course and breaking down.

Podium position
Paul Newman in the Porsche
935, which got him to second
place in Le Mans in 1979.

In 1978, Newman founded a racing team that
would go on to compete in motor racing right
through to the present day, and which helped the
likes of Mario Andretti, Nigel Mansell and
Sébastien Bourdais to championship wins in the
US Champ Car series.

Newman never stopped working, or getting
involved with cars. At the age of 70, he took third
place in the 24 Hours of Daytona. As an actor, he
appeared in sixty films, and was director of six.
And his final film work, at the age of 83,
combined both cars and films, as the voice of
Doc Hudson, the old Hudson Hornet in the
animated film *Cars* (2006).

Despite their common passion for racing,
McQueen and Newman were never really friends.
In fact, their relationship was marked by rivalry,
especially when they worked together. During the
filming of *The Towering Inferno* in 1974, McQueen
(who rose to fame later than Newman, and who
found Newman less than friendly on set during
an earlier film collaboration) had negotiated that
the two star actors would have *exactly* the same
number of scenes. Motor racing fans can only
regret that these rivalries were played out only in
the cinema – and not on the racetrack. That
would have been an event worth seeing.

PORSCHE
911 S 1969

ENGINE
Configuration **6-cylinder, flat-six**
Capacity **1991 cc**
Fuel **Petrol**
Layout **Rear engine, longitudinal**

TRANSMISSION
Gearbox **5-speed, manual**
Drive type **Rear wheel drive**

DIMENSIONS
Length **4.41 m** / Width **1.61 m**
Height **1.32 m**
Weight **1050 kg**

PERFORMANCE
Power **160 bhp**
Maximum speed **140 mph**

① Perfect compromise

Less expensive than the Italian sports cars, and more modern-looking than the British roadsters, the Porsche 911 was the perfect compromise – with an exceptional power-to-weight ratio for great performance.

② A winning design

Launched in 1963, the 911 went through multiple re-stylings over the years, but retained the same basic layout underneath for more than three decades. A common and defining feature was the engine: the air-cooled flat-6 with its characteristic rorty growl.

③ Team racer

The Porsche 911 S 1969 was one of the first cars to be raced by the Newman-Freeman team. Later, Newman himself favoured the motorsport derivatives, such as the 935 he drove at Le Mans.

④ The power of six

The 911 was the first Porsche to be fitted with a six-cylinder motor (the 912 had a four-cylinder engine) and it was on the racetrack that Porsche was able to show the world the capability of this bigger and more powerful engine.

AND THE REST
ACTORS AND RACERS

'AT THE 24 HOURS OF LE MANS, I CAME OFF THE TRACK AT 325 KILOMETRES PER HOUR. I WAS LUCKY: THE CAR SLAMMED FROM ONE CRASH BARRIER TO THE OTHER SIX TIMES IN A ROW, BUT NEVER HIT HEAD ON.'

JEAN-LOUIS TRINTIGNANT

Steve McQueen and Paul Newman, the two biggest American stars of the 1970s, were both accomplished racing drivers. But this combination of skills – acting and racing – is quite a rarity. Plenty of actors liked to play at being racing drivers on screen, or pose in front of racecars for the cameras. But successful motorsport demands an obsessional level of commitment, which very few actors are able to make. So who else is there that has managed to combine both? From the US, there is the actor James Coburn, a friend of McQueen, and co-star with McQueen in *The Magnificent Seven* in 1960 and *The Great Escape* in 1963. Coburn was the son of a motor mechanic, became a collector of various Ferraris, and raced in his free time. Meanwhile, in Europe, the most celebrated actor-racer is Jean-Louis Trintignant. The French actor took on the role of a racing driver in Claude Lelouch's Palme d'Or and Oscar Award-winning film *A Man and a Woman*. The film not only helped put the chic beach resort of Deauville on the international map, but it also did a lot for the European sales of the Ford Mustang. In the film, Trintignant drives a 1965 Mustang coupé (the model preceding the Fastback version driven by McQueen in *Bullitt*.) There were no adrenaline-fuelled car chases in this cerebral French drama filmed in black and white. But Trintignant did start a new trend of shaving while driving (much imitated, but not to be recommended), using an electric razor at the wheel of his Mustang as he headed south to hook up with co-star Anouk Aimée. Trintignant himself had, to some degree, petrol running through his blood: he was the nephew of Formula 1 driver Maurice Trintignant, and had grown up around fast cars, racetracks and the paddock. As part of his preparation for *A Man and a Woman*, he hung out with Formula 1 champion Jean-Pierre Beltoise, and later tried out motor racing himself. This started in the 1970s with the Star Racing Team, which had a series of races in

JEAN-LOUIS TRINTIGNANT
A MAN AND A WOMAN (1966)
Ford Mustang 1965

STEVE MCQUEEN
LE MANS (1971)
Porsche 917

BRASSEUR, TRINTIGNANT
STAR RACING TEAM 1975
Simca 1000

souped-up but diminutive Simca 1000s, driven by celebrities – mainly French actors and singers, including Claude Brasseur, Guy Marchand and Johnny Hallyday. It was here that Trintignan met the racing driver Marianne Hoepfner - who later became his wife – and with whom he took part in the Monte Carlo Rally in 1981 and 1982, as well as the 24 Hours of Spa-Francorchamps in 1981, where they finished a creditable seventh place. Trintignant also raced in the 24 Hours of Le Mans in 1980 and the Bandama Rally on the Ivory Coast in 1981 with Porsche (935 and 924). Another alumni of Star Racing Team, the actor Claude Brasseur (whose film credits include *The Party* and *The Supper*) had been navigator with Belgian champion driver Jacky Ickx over six Paris-Dakar rallies, winning the event in 1983. And rather more recently, you can also include Patrick Dempsey, who plays Dr Derek Shepherd in *Grey's Anatomy*.

He put together a racing team in 2002, entering Ferrari and Porsche in various championships, competing three times at Le Mans, and finishing in third place in the 24 Hours of Daytona in 2011. Dempsey, then, carries the torch for the tradition of the American actor-racer, even if he retains somewhat less of a following than the stars of *Winning* (Newman) or *Le Mans* (McQueen).

Star on a car
Actor Jean-Louis Trintignant on the bonnet of a Simca 1000 in the Star Racing Team series, which got him seriously into motorsport.

JEAN-LOUIS TRINTIGNANT
24 H OF MANS 1980
Porsche 935 K3 Kremer

BRASSEUR-ICKX
PARIS-DAKAR 1983
Mercedes Class G

PATRICK DEMPSEY
24 H OF DAYTONA 2011
Porsche 911 GT3

GENTLEMEN

JAMES BOND ASTON MARTIN DB5 1964

ROGER MOORE ASTON MARTIN DBS 1970

ROGER MOORE AND SPORTS CARS

ALAIN DELON FERRARI 250 GT CALIFORNIA SPYDER SWB 1961

MARCELLO MASTROIANNI TRIUMPH TR3A 1958

DRIVERS 2

'NOW, PAY ATTENTION PLEASE. WINDSCREEN -
BULLETPROOF. AS ARE THE SIDE AND THE REAR
WINDOWS. REVOLVING NUMBER PLATES,
NATURALLY. VALID - ALL COUNTRIES.'

Q IN *GOLDFINGER* (1964)

JAMES BOND
& ASTON MARTIN

DB5 1964

Sean Connery on the set of
Goldfinger (1964), the first
Bond film to feature the
legendary Aston Martin DB5.

Over the decades, the James Bond actors changed, the costumes moved on with the times, and even the recipe for a Dry Martini has evolved (in the most recent films, gin is replaced by vodka). But the Aston Martin of the 1960s, designed by Italian coachbuilder Touring, and appearing in a succession of Bond films across the decades, remains the most celebrated cult car in cinematic history.

In the original Ian Fleming novels, Bond drove an Aston Martin DB2/4 Mark III. However, the very first 'Bond Car' in the film series, featured in *From Russia With Love* (1963) was a massive Bentley 4½ from 1930 (the same model that John Steed used to drive in *The Avengers*). Fleming wrote that while the Aston was Bond's 'company car', the Bentley was 'his only personal hobby'.

In subsequent films, Astons were always close to the action. A DBS in *On Her Majesty's Secret Service* (1969); A V8 in *The Living Daylights* (1987), one of just two Bond films with Timothy Dalton. And a DBS V12 was the star of the jaw-dropping car chase that opens *Quantum of Solace* (2008) with Daniel Craig. James Bond is Aston Martin. Aston Martin is James Bond.

For the filming of *Spectre* (2015), Aston Martin built a completely new model of the DB10 in a limited run of just ten cars, to mark the fifty-year

The Living Daylights
The arrival of Timothy Dalton in the role of Bond for *The Living Daylights* (1987) also saw the return of Aston Martin to the Bond franchise – and this time, it looks set to stay.

partnership between the carmaker and the Bond films. The all-carbon bodywork was finished in Silver Birch paintwork – the iconic colour of the DB5s that featured in so many of the earlier Bond films, including *GoldenEye* (1995), which marked the arrival of Pierce Brosnan as 007, as well as *Casino Royale* (2006) – the first episode of Bond for Daniel Craig. Straying from the Aston Martin brand has not played so well with diehard Bond fans. In *The Spy Who Loved Me* (1978), Bond was handed the keys to a Lotus Esprit, which did however win approval for its capability as a submarine. In any case, Moore, the 007 at the time, preferred skiing to driving: the film began with the amazing ski pursuit sequence between Bond and KGB agents, culminating in Bond skiing off a cliff and opening up a Union Jack parachute. With this in mind, at the start of *For Your Eyes Only* (1981), when Bond's Lotus Esprit was blown to pieces in an explosion, Q produced a replacement Lotus, in red and gold, and fitted, conveniently for Moore, with a ski rack.

Die Another Day
Pierce Brosnan is introduced
to his Aston Martin Vanquish
in *Die Another Day* (2002) in
front of Q (John Cleese), whose
main concern is whether the
car will come back in one piece.

A German affair

If the relationship between Aston Martin and
the Bond films over the years was like a marriage,
then the partnership with BMW during the 1990s
was seen by some fans as a major act of infidelity.
Pierce Brosnan's Bond drove Aston Martins as his
personal car, but his 'company cars' were a fleet
of BMWs: the 750iL, the Z3, and even the
helicopter-jumping R1200C motorcycle featured
in *Tomorrow Never Dies* in 1997.

Despite the appearance of the very classy Z8
in *The World Is Not Enough* (1999), the idea of
the quintessentially British James Bond driving a
German car unsettled many traditional Bond
fans. The old order did, however, return in later
films, but with subtle changes. Daniel Craig's
Bond wears American suits from Tom Ford, and
the Astons he drives are from a British carmaker
owned by a Kuwaiti investment fund. But the
pairing of Bond and Aston Martin is ever-present.
In the final scene of *Spectre*, Daniel Craig and
co-star Léa Seydoux drive off in the classic DB5
– with passenger ejector seat as standard.

'OH, AND I SUPPOSE THAT'S COMPLETELY INCONSPICUOUS.'
M TO JAMES BOND IN *SKYFALL* (2012)

Skyfall (2012)
Daniel Craig's third billing as Bond

ASTON MARTIN
1964 DB5

ENGINE
Configuration **6-cylinder, in-line**
Capacity **3996 cc**
Fuel **Petrol**
Layout **Front engine, longitudinal**

TRANSMISSION
Gearbox **5-speed, manual**
Drive type **Rear wheel drive**

DIMENSIONS
Length **4.57 m** / Width **1.68 m**
Height **1.38 m**
Weight **1465 kg**

PERFORMANCE
Power **286 bhp**
Maximum speed **143 mph**

① The mixed grille

The oval grille of the Aston Martin is neither horizontal nor vertical in style, but seems to exist somewhere between the two, in perfect balance with the car's inspired design.

② Mini-evolution for maxi effect

The single biggest difference between the DB5 and its forerunner the DB4 is in the headlights. The DB4's were upright, encased in fairings leading off the wing. The DB5 lights are raked back and recessed. A mini-evolution, perhaps, but one that manages to transform an elegant GT car into a classic sports model.

③ Signature detail

First seen on the DB4, the air outlet with the chrome bar running through it became a signature detail of the marque, and is found on all Astons right through to the DB 11 launched in 2016.

④ British traditions

With chrome bodywork, spoked wheels and a steering wheel in riveted wood, Aston Martin brought together the traditional features of the British sports car with the sensuous styling of the Italian studio Touring.

Riviera Style
Two playboys and an Aston Martin on the Côte d'Azur: how to add serious glamour to a police action series.

ROGER MOORE
& ASTON MARTIN

DBS 1970

In *The Persuaders!* (1971-72), the opening sequence presents two possible routes to wealth. With a John Barry signature theme playing in the background, the screen image splits in two, and you watch the backstories playing out in black and white in the lives of Lord Brett Sinclair (Roger Moore) on one side of the screen, and of Danny Wilde (Tony Curtis) on the other. On Sinclair's side, you see the best public schools of England, and the life of a sporting hero who rises to the top in Formula One racing. On the Wilde side, as it were, you can see a childhood spent surviving on the streets, followed by a life as a huckster and dealmaker, which propelled Danny Wilde to the top as an oil magnate. The sequence finishes with a car chase through narrow streets on the French Riviera. Sinclair drives an Aston Martin DBS in an immaculate deep orange (just like that of George Lazenby, in *On Her Majesty's Secret Service* in 1969). Wilde is in a bright red Dino 246 GT.

Sinclair and Wilde, Aston and Dino, are poles apart. The classic and understated English car oozing 'old money' and privilege, versus the noisy Italian driven by the fast-talking 'new money' New Yorker.

Sixties design
An English car, designed in Italy by Touring in 1967, and which went on to inspire the Mustang and the Charger in the US. Note the flashy mustard paintwork, as the famous British reserve starts to go 'pop'.

The contrast was spot-on. The Dino (named in memory of Enzo Ferrari's son) was developed to be a more accessible Ferrari, pitched to rival the success of cars like the Porsche 911. It was, after all, very different from the classic Ferraris, with its berlinetta body style and mid-engine layout. And the engine itself was a relatively modest six-cylinder unit – a motor developed originally for the top-end range of Fiat, which was now the owner of the Ferrari marque.

In the film, Sinclair and Wilde are brought together by a retired judge who recruits the two idle playboys to help him bring criminals to justice. The pair learns to overcome their differences and take a liking to each other – something that cannot be said for the two actors in real life, who did not get on enormously well on set.

Meanwhile, despite the 'old money' status of the Aston DBS in the film, in real life both the car and the *Persuaders!* series were somewhat in the shadow of the Aston DB5 and the Bond franchise. At auction in Newport Pagnell in May 2014, the Aston of Lord Brett Sinclair from the TV series was sold for £533,000. Four years earlier, the DB5 of James Bond went under the hammer for more than *five times* this amount.

ROGER MOORE
& SPORTS CARS

'SEAN LOOKS AS THOUGH HE WANTS TO KILL THE VILLAIN. DANIEL YOU *KNOW* IS GOING TO KILL THE VILLAIN, WHEREAS I LOOK AS IF I WANT TO HUG THEM, OR BORE THEM TO DEATH.'

ROGER MOORE

Roger Moore made his British TV debut in 1958 with the series *Ivanhoe*. Loosely based around the novel by Walter Scott, this epic set in the Middle Ages saw Moore clad in armour, riding on horseback. It was another three years before he could be seen wearing a bespoke suit and driving a sports car – as he was to go on doing for much of his future career. In the TV series *The Saint* (1962-69), he played an adventurer, vigilante, and playboy, all of which hinted at the direction his future acting career would take. In *The Saint*, Moore spent a lot of time driving a Volvo P1800 coupé (1961-1973) designed in Italy by Pietro Frua, and representing a fascinating mix of Italian styling on the outside, and robust Swedish engineering underneath. In fact it was a P1800 that held a world endurance record: an American model was recorded as having covered the incredible distance of 3 *million* miles.

The success of Moore's role in *The Saint* was such that by the end of the 1960s, he chose to turn down, on two occasions, the chance to become James Bond. Instead, he moved on to *The Persuaders!*, where he took on the role of the quintessential English aristocrat, driving the latest, and most fashionable Aston Martin. (In real life, Moore's own background was more modest – his father was a policeman.)

At the start of the 1970s, he was again offered the role of Bond, and this time he accepted. Moore joined at an interesting time. After the somewhat lukewarm reaction to Sean Connery's immediate successor George Lazenby (*On Her Majesty's Secret Service*, 1969), MGM wanted to make a few changes. So the dry Martinis were out, to be replaced by bourbon. Instead of a Rolex, the wristwatch would be Seiko. And the biggest change of all: the Aston Martin was ousted in favour of the Lotus Esprit. The Esprit was a typical 1970s sports

---

THE SAINT (1962-1969)
Volvo P1800

THE PERSUADERS! (1971)
Aston Martin coupé DBS

THE SPY WHO LOVED ME (1977)
Lotus Esprit

coupe, mid-engined and turbocharged, and with striking angular bodywork styled by Giorgetto Giugiaro – the man who had designed the iconic VW Golf, and even the DeLorean as seen in *Back To The Future* (1985). Die-hard Aston Martin fans may have been a tad disappointed by the appearance of a Lotus – but perhaps less so when it proved it was capable of transforming itself into a

submarine in *The Spy Who Loved Me* (1977). For Roger Moore, the Lotus was the only sports car he drove in the Bond films. After a second Lotus Esprit is blown up at the start of *For Your Eyes Only* (1981), the ensuing car chase sees Bond driving the Citroen 2CV belonging to Melina Havelock (Carole Bouquet). Four years on, in *View To Kill* (1985) the action takes place with Bond in exactly

one half of a Renault 11 (which has been sliced in two). None of this bothered Roger Moore. Two decades later, he told interviewers that the car he had enjoyed driving more than any other during his lifetime was his 1960s Volvo in *The Saint*.

Moore's Law

In *For Your Eyes Only* (1981) James Bond is back in a Lotus Esprit, this time a Turbo version, and with a subtle red and gold paint job. Unlike its predecessor, it was not submersible. But it did have a ski rack.

ALAIN DELON
& FERRARI
250 GT CALIFORNIA SPYDER SWB 1961

Joy House
Alain Delon and Jane Fonda in his Ferrari Spyder, on the set of *Joy House*, 1964. Delon did not believe that the identical-looking Spyder, discovered in a barn decades later, was the same car. Nobody wanted to believe him.

In the 1960s, Alain Delon had owned several Ferraris, including a magnificent 250 GT California Spyder that featured in the filming of *Joy House* (1964) with Jane Fonda. Some fifty years later, the car appeared to have been rediscovered in a barn (covered in a pile of old magazines), and went on to be sold at auction for 14 million euros at Artcurial in Paris. An amazing sum of money, but the 250 California really is the quintessential 'car of the stars': an elegant cabriolet with lusciously curved bodywork, built by Ferrari at the request of its importers in the USA. The design was from Pininfarina, bodywork by Scaglietti, and power came from a 3l V12 – with only one hundred models produced between 1958 and 1962. In fact, the short-wheelbase version driven by Delon is even more rare: only 27 models were ever made. Despite, or maybe because of its rarity, this exclusive car became famous worldwide, and it's worth wondering if any of these 27 models has *not* passed through the hands of one celebrity or another over the last fifty years. Ferrari collector and race driver James Coburn (*The Magnificent Seven*, 1960) owned one, which was subsequently sold in 2008 for 7 million euros to British TV presenter Chris Evans. In France, the

My other car is a Spyder
As well as the legendary California Spyder, Alain Delon owned and drove a number of other Ferrari models in the 1960s, including this elegant 250 GT Cabriolet.

author Francoise Sagan and singer Johnny Hallyday also owned 250s, and film director Roger Vadim (*And God Created Woman,* 1956; *Barbarella,* 1968) sold his Spyder in 2012 for 4.5 million euros. More recently, Nicolas Cage added a California to his own collection.

Alain Delon himself drove rather more mainstream Italian cars in his films during the 1960s and 1970s. There was an Alfa Romeo (*Eclipse,* 1962, *Any Number Can Win,* 1963, *Death Of A Corrupt Man,* 1977) and then in the 1980s several Lancia models (*Three Men To Kill,* 1980, *Let Sleeping Cops Lie,* 1988). In fact, Delon was a friend of André Chardonnet, who was importing Lancia into France at that time. All his life, Delon owned a BMW, and in more recent years, he has made plenty of use of the so-called 'Vélib' – the free bicycles available on the streets of central Paris. Delon spent some time living in Italy, and his image remains closely linked with Italian sports cars such as the Maserati Ghibli, which he drives briefly in the film *The Swimming Pool* (1969). In 2011, that driving sequence re-appeared in an advertisement for Dior's perfume Eau Sauvage, playing on the Ghibli's image of strength and refinement, and reflecting the aura surrounding Alain Delon himself.

FERRARI
1961 250 GT CALIFORNIA SPYDER SWB

ENGINE
Configuration **12-cylinder, V12**
Capacity **2953 cc**
Fuel **Petrol**
Layout **Front engine, longitudinal**

TRANSMISSION
Gearbox **4-speed, manual**
Drive type **Rear wheel drive**

DIMENSIONS
Length **4.20 m** / Width **1.72 m**
Height **1.37 m**
Weight **1050 kg**

PERFORMANCE
Power **280 bhp**
Maximum speed **155 mph**

ARTCURIAL
MOTORCARS

④

① American Dream

The California cabriolet was created at the request of the US importers – notably John von Neumann in California and Luigi Chinetti in New York. It was this kind of strong and country-specific demand that also led to the creation of the Porsche 356 Speedster.

② Film credits

In the 1980s, the California made a come-back thanks to its appearance in two films: *The Flamingo Kid*, in 1984 with Matt Dillon, and two years later in *Ferris Bueller's Day Off*, starring Matthew Broderick.

③ Not Just In Red

Ferraris are closely associated with their trademark red paintwork, which happens to be their racing colour. The California was sold in plenty of other colours too: dark green for James Coburn, black for Alain Delon and Nicholas Cage, and metallic grey for Roger Vadim.

④ Classic GT styling

Faired-in headlights, long bonnet, air scoops in the front wings: from 1958, Pininfarina made sure the California had all the essential styling features that would guarantee the success of the 1960s GT cars like E-Type Jaguar, Aston Martin DB5 and Ferrari 275 GTB.

MARCELLO MASTROIANNI
& TRIUMPH
TR3A 1958

La Dolce Vita
Marcello Mastroianni and
Triumph TR3A in Federico
Fellini's *La Dolce Vita* (1960).

In *Il Sorpasso,* a 1962 film by Dino Risi, a Lancia
Aurelia Spider is sent plunging off a cliff. In the
same year, in the film *L'Eclisse* by Michelangelo
Antonioni, Alain Delon drives an Alfa Romeo
Giulietta Cabriolet – which ends up at the bottom
of the river Tiber. While Italian cinema was ready
to trash some beautiful cars in the 1960s, it was
also very much in love with them. Filmed in black
and white, the protagonists worked through their
existential crises while wearing elegant suits and
driving fabulous sports cars. Curiously, in the film
that came to symbolise this era across the world
– Fellini's *La Dolce Vita* – it is a British roadster, a
1958 Triumph TR3A, that Marcello Mastroianni
uses to drive from one glamorous Roman party
to another. So we watch the high society gossip
columnist driving through a hot and humid
summer night, looking for celebrities and scandal,
and trailed by his paparazzi colleagues on
scooters or Fiat 500s. In 1953, in *Roman Holiday*,
Gregory Peck and Audrey Hepburn showed the
American public the streets of the eternal city as
they crisscrossed Rome on a Vespa. Since then,
Italy seemed to become the prize destination of
the world's rich, and idle rich.

It's worth noting that in addition to the British
Triumph TR3, Italian cinema also welcomed

La Dolce Vita
In Fellini's film, jaded society journalist Marcello fills his Triumph TR3 with partygoers that he hardly knows, and drives them from one luxury villa to another.

plenty of actors and technicians from abroad. In *La Dolce Vita*, Mastroianni meets the French actress Anouk Aimée (in a Cadillac), as well as Nico, a German model (in the back of a Rolls-Royce) and the Swedish actress Anita Ekberg, playing an American star, in the famous scene in the Trevi fountain. Marcello's choice of car, a Triumph from England, is symptomatic of this openness to the world. Rome is in the process of inventing the jet set, of which the uncontested prince was to be Giovanni Agnelli, the boss of Fiat, who would go on to buy out both Ferrari and Lancia. Agnelli himself was typically seen driving bespoke Pininfarina-styled versions of cars that were part of his automotive empire. As for Marcello Mastroianni, he also had a passion for beautiful cars when he was not on screen, most notably a magnificent 1966 Lancia Flaminia Supersport Zagato. Fellini shared this passion, almost in competition with the actor, and at one time owned a Flaminia Cabrio, an imposing 4-door convertible which happened to be the model chosen as the official car of the Italian president. In 1963, Mastroianni played the part of a film director in the film *8½*, bearing a striking similarity to Fellini himself – a character bored by his sedate Lancia, but in much better mood driving a Porsche 356.

TRIUMPH
TR3A 1958

ENGINE
Configuration **4-cylinder, in line**
Capacity **1991 cc**
Fuel **Petrol**
Layout **Front engine, longitudinal**

TRANSMISSION
Gearbox **4-speed, manual with overdrive**
Drive type **Rear wheel drive**

DIMENSIONS
Length **3.83 m** / Width **1.42 m**
Height **1.27 m**
Weight **948 kg**

PERFORMANCE
Power **100 bhp**
Maximum speed **106 mph**

① Tractor power

The Standard Vanguard 4-cylinder engine under the bonnet of the TR3 is, believe it or not, the same motor that is found in the classic Massey Ferguson tractors. With the addition of carburetors and a more refined camshaft, it remains a fairly agricultural piece of engineering – but sounds amazing.

② True Brit

With the MGA and the Austin-Healey, the Triumph is a quintessential classic English roadster. An indestructible motor and minimalist bodywork put them at the opposite end of the spectrum in comparison with their sophisticated German and Italian rivals.

③ Export grade

It's not too surprising that the TR3 featured in *La Dolce Vita*, as some 95% of the production of the TR3 was built for export. In the USA, its biggest market, the price was $2,500 – a full $1,000 less than American rivals such as the Corvette or Thunderbird.

④ Mind the doors

The cabin of the TR3 has extremely low doors, to the point that most of its drivers don't even take the trouble of opening them. They just climb straight over.

FOOT TO THE

MAD MAX FORD FALCON 'V8 INTERCEPTOR' 1973

THE BLUES BROTHERS DODGE MONACO 1974 'BLUESMOBILE'

POLICE CARS TRASHED AND THRASHED BY AMERICAN CINEMA

VIN DIESEL DODGE CHARGER R/T 1969

RYAN GOSLING CHEVROLET CHEVELLE MALIBU SS 1973

MICHAEL CAINE AUSTIN MINI COOPER S MK II 1967

ROBBERIES AT THE WHEEL

FLOOR 3

MAD MAX
& FORD FALCON
'V8 INTERCEPTOR' 1973

'IN THE ROAR OF AN ENGINE, HE LOST EVERYTHING ... AND BECAME A SHELL OF A MAN ... A BURNT-OUT, DESOLATE MAN, A MAN HAUNTED BY THE DEMONS OF HIS PAST, A MAN WHO WANDERED OUT INTO THE WASTELAND.'

MAD MAX 2, PROLOGUE

In American cinema, according to director Quentin Tarantino, audiences tend to experience car chases 'like bystanders in a town'. If that is so, then you could say that in Australian films, the audience gets to witness the chase from a totally different viewpoint: strapped into the front passenger seat. At least that is how it looks in George Miller's *Mad Max* films – distinguished not only for the quality of the chase sequences, but also for the vehicle that

launched a star of global calibre: Mel Gibson. The *Mad Max* leviathan started out as a B-movie on a small budget in 1979 – so small in fact, that the costume budget only ran to one outfit made from genuine leather (worn by Max) and had to use fake leather for the rest of the cast. Max Rockatansky, the eponymous Mad Max, is a traffic cop who takes on a band of bikers to avenge the death of his wife and his son. And his car? The V8 Interceptor, also known as 'Pursuit Special', a specially prepped Australian 1973 Ford Falcon. It was a vehicle completely unknown to the rest of the world, but one that was about to gain cult status.

Building on its international success, *Mad Max 2: The Road Warrior* followed in 1981, with a budget some ten times higher. And then a third, though a little less inspiring: *Mad Max Beyond Thunderdome* in 1985.

Road Warriors
The *Mad Max* movies rolled
out a jaw-dropping series of
stripped down, mashed-up and
heavily armoured cars, trucks,
and bikes. *Mad Max: Fury Road*
pushed this art to the limits.

Mel Gibson became the world's number one
action movie star, and garnered more career
success with the cult series of films *Lethal Weapon*
before moving into directing (with credits
including *Braveheart* and *Apocalypto*). And just
when nobody was expecting it, George Miller
returned as producer to *Mad Max: Fury Road* in
2015, to international critical acclaim. The vehicles
were more extreme than ever, and Miller gave free
rein to his fertile imagination, welding vintage
bodywork to the chassis of trucks to create an
extraordinary motorized convoy beyond the realm
of dreams or nightmares. The English actor Tom
Hardy replaced Gibson as Max, but the Interceptor
remained, and with the chase sequences even
more spectacular.

FORD
1973 FALCON 'V8 INTERCEPTOR'

ENGINE
Configuration **8-cylinder, V8**
Capacity **5.8 litres**
Fuel **Petrol**
Layout **Front engine, longitudinal**

TRANSMISSION
Gearbox **4-speed, manual**
Drive type **Rear wheel drive**

DIMENSIONS
Length **4.80 m** / Width **1.95 m**
Height **1.29 m**
Weight **1394 kg**

PERFORMANCE
Power **400 bhp**
Maximum speed **174 mph (aided by supercharger and fuel additives)**

1 A look much copied

Hundreds of owners of Ford Falcons (and in the US, Ford Mustangs and in the UK, Ford Capris) tried to transform their cars into the Interceptor, with mixed results, from the good, to the bad, to the plain ugly. In Australia, the Ford Falcon became a cult car in its original, unmodified version.

2 A car on steroids

Max's car was equipped with a supercharger, with the enormous air intake protruding through the bonnet, and multiple exhausts positioned to the sides of the car. The 400 bhp 5.8 l V8 could get the car up to 175 mph, thanks to a high octane fuel supplement as used in dragster racing.

3 Spoiler personality

Spoilers on the roof and bonnet provide down force, but the modification to the front of the car – effectively a nose cone and air dam – lent the car an unmistakable 'face'.

4 Aussie muscle car

The Falcon was specific to Ford Australia, and had been built in 2-door and 4-door versions since the 1960s. The coupé XB GT Falcon Hardtop, manufactured from 1973 to 1976, resembled the American Mustang Mach 1, apart from some styling on the rear wings. It was this model that formed

THE BLUES BROTHERS

& DODGE

MONACO 1974 'BLUESMOBILE'

'IT'S 106 MILES TO CHICAGO, WE GOT A
FULL TANK OF GAS, HALF A PACK OF CIGARETTES,
IT'S DARK ... AND WE'RE WEARING SUNGLASSES.'

THE BLUES BROTHERS, (1980)

The scene is familiar: two men in dark suits, white shirts and black ties, one behind the wheel of a black and white police cruiser, the other sitting to his right in the passenger seat. With a soundtrack playing the best of soul music from Ray Charles, to Aretha Franklin, to James Brown, you could be watching a crime movie from the 1960s. Except something's not quite right: it's dark outside, and the two of them are wearing sunglasses. And behind them, strung out on the road, dozens of police cars are giving chase. That, in essence, is *The Blues Brothers*. The two stars of this iconic comedy, John Belushi and Dan Aykroyd, rose to fame on the US comedy weekly TV show *Saturday Night Live*, where they poked fun at the white fans of soul music. Following this, director John Landis got the idea to make a film – a musical film – about the Blues Brothers, Jake Blues (Belushi) and his brother Elwood (Aykroyd) travelling between gigs and being pursued not only by the police, but also by the American Nazi party. At one point, Jake's vengeful ex-fiancé, played by Carrie Fisher, fires at him with an M16 rifle from the window of a 1977 Pontiac Grand Prix.

Jake and Elwood's car – the 'Bluesmobile' – is a 1974 Dodge Monaco (with a specially adapted engine, shock absorbers and suspension). In the film, this becomes an ex-police cruiser ready for

Blues Brothers 2000
In 1998 John Landis created a sequel, with Dan Aykroyd playing alongside John Goodman, J. Evan Bonifant and Joe Morton (right). The musical score was just as good (BB King, Wilson Pickett, James Brown), but the chase sequences not a patch on the original (below).

the scrap heap, bought by Elwood in exchange for a loaf of bread, having sold their old Cadillac to buy a new microphone. Ultimately, the police cruiser turned out to be exactly what they needed to escape from their pursuers. During filming, an astonishing sixty 'standard' police cruisers were destroyed in the action sequences, along with a dozen models of the Bluesmobile. This was a record for any car chase in any film that endured for the next twenty years (when it was surpassed by GI Joe). Perhaps the most extraordinary chase sequence is the one in a shopping mall, which ends up in total devastation. John Landis and Dan Aykroyd came together later to create a sequel in 1998 (Blues Brothers 2000), but sadly without John Belushi – who died of a drugs overdose in Hollywood at the age of 33.

POLICE CARS
TRASHED AND THRASHED BY AMERICAN CINEMA

Newman the cop
Paul Newman trades in his Porsche for a Plymouth as he takes on the role of a beat officer in *Fort Apache, The Bronx* (1981).

While the Blues Brothers is one of the films that destroyed the greatest number of police cars, the act of trashing police cars has a long tradition in US films. A good number of chase sequences are a kind of cheerful parody of those seen in earlier films such as William Friedkin's *The French Connection* (1971) among many others. But if there are plenty of police cars in American films, the stars of the films are rarely driving them. There are just a handful of exceptions: Paul Newman drove a Plymouth Fury in *Fort Apache, The Bronx* in 1981; Robert Duvall and Sean Penn patrolled Los Angeles in a two-tone Chevrolet Impala in *Colors* (1988); and twenty years later, Jake Gyllenhaal drove through the same streets in a Ford Crown Victoria (*End of Watch*) in 2012. Ted Kotcheff's 1982 *Rambo: First Blood*, starring Sylvester Stallone, is typical of the role played by the police car in US fiction. Brian Dennehy, sheriff of a small town in the Rocky Mountains, is on patrol in a blue and white 1977 Ford LTD II, when he sees Rambo, walking alone down the highway. On the lookout for drifters and troublemakers, Dennehy obliges Rambo to get into the patrol car to drive him out of town. Rambo, of course, is not best pleased. This goes to illustrate, not only that police jurisdictions can be strictly local, but also that their cars, and even the colours in which they are painted, are part of the identity of each town, however big or small. In the comedy *Beverly Hills Cop* (1984), Detroit police officer Eddy Murphy finds himself arrested in an upmarket LA suburb, and is

amazed at how the squad car is immaculately clean, compared with the filthy old rust-buckets he has to drive in Michigan.

In most films, though, cop cars are seen only from a distance: usually driving en masse in pursuit, plunging into ravines, or sliding to a halt on their roof.

The Hollywood mythology of Rambo (and hundreds of other films) is hard to escape: a lone man (and usually a man) fighting against 'the system', with that system symbolised by the forces of law and order. Not surprising, then, that Hollywood

has never played up the driving skills of the police officers at the wheel of these cars. The pattern was set very early in cinematic history. In the detective films from Warner in the 1930s, Edward G Robinson (*Little Caesar*, 1931) and James Cagney (*The Public Enemy*, 1931) manage to wreak havoc among the police's Model A or Model B Fords of the time, just as we might see today with Dom Toretto's gang causing chaos among the massed vehicles of the forces of law in *Fast and Furious*. And from the 1930s

right through to the present day, there are hundreds of other examples of the genre. To mention just two: *Smokey and the Bandit* in 1977 with Burt Reynolds, and *The Fifth Element* with Bruce Willis (the latter film just goes to show that even in a science fiction movie directed by a Frenchman, the American-born conventions of the car chase are dutifully observed.) So in a world of cars and stars, across five generations of Hollywood movies, the police patrol car has always been a kind of sacrificial victim.

Joker on patrol
A police car is stolen by the Joker (Heath Ledger) in *The Dark Knight* (2008).

LITTLE CAESAR (1931)
Ford A

RAMBO (1982)
Ford LTD II 1977

END OF WATCH (2012)
Ford Crown Victoria 1999

VIN DIESEL
& DODGE
CHARGER R/T 1969

Supercharged
The distinctive air intake
of the supercharger on
Dom's trademark 1969
Dodge Charger R/T.

When *Fast and Furious* was released in 2001, it was with modest expectations for what was an action movie with a relatively moderate ($38m) budget. The scenario was predictable enough: a police officer goes undercover in a gang of street racers suspected of organizing a string of robberies. The principal actors, Vin Diesel and Paul Walker, were respectable action movie stars, and that was about it. But the film was an instant commercial success, with box office receipts five times the budget. The second instalment was also a hit, despite the departure of Diesel, as was the third (with the departure, this time, of Paul Walker.) Both actors came back to make *Fast and Furious 4, 5* and *6,* which managed to extend the action to different continents and help ensure box office receipts across the entire globe. The seventh *Fast and Furious* was released in 2015, and brought in more than $1.5 billion (matching the kind of revenue from the likes of *The Avengers* or *Star Wars*). And despite the tragic death of Paul Walker in a road accident in 2013, the series looks set to continue. For one thing, it seems to communicate with car enthusiasts the world over. Beyond the basic physical antagonism of its protagonists, it also features a kind of automotive conflict that is instantly recognisable and which is

VIN DIESEL & DODGE CHARGER R/T 1969

Splash!
In the opening sequence of *Fast and Furious 5*, Paul Walker and Vin Diesel drive off a cliff in a 1963 Corvette Grand Sport.

the key to the majority of the chase scenes. Dom Toretto (played by the shaven-headed Vin Diesel), the gang leader, favours heavyweight American muscle cars, with their V8 engines and electrifying acceleration: cars like the Chryslers from the 1960s – the Dodge Charger or Challenger, the Plymouth Barracuda and so on. Meanwhile, undercover cop Brian O'Conner (who was played by Walker), prefers small but agile Japanese coupés, stuffed with smart technology. This 'brains versus brawn' scenario, where the cars in some way take on, or add to, the character of their drivers, is seen in plenty of other movies too – such as *The Persuaders!* and *The Avengers*, but has never been more obvious than in *Fast and Furious*. Every wannabe street racer, or indeed every 'driver' of a games console, identifies with one or the other of the two camps, and follows the film with the same kind of passion as a football fan.

DODGE
1969 CHARGER R/T

ENGINE
Configuration **8-cylinder, V8 'Hemi' Big Block**
Capacity **7.2 litres**
Fuel **Petrol**
Layout **Front engine, longitudinal**

TRANSMISSION
Gearbox **4-speed, manual**
Drive type **Rear wheel drive**

DIMENSIONS
Length **5.17 m** / Width **1.91 m**
Height **1.32 m**
Weight **1891 kg**

PERFORMANCE
Power **425 bhp**
Maximum speed **137 mph**

① The mythical V8

Built by the Chrysler Group, America's third largest manufacturer (behind Ford and General Motors), the Dodge is equipped with a V8-Hemi (a hemi-spherical combustion chamber, in fact), derived from the legendary motor of the Chrysler 300 from the 1950s.

② One for the bad guys

The Dodge Charger is also the car of Steve McQueen's adversaries in *Bullitt*, and of the Duke boys in *The Dukes of Hazzard*. No surprise, then, that this should become the preferred wheels for the criminal gang in *Fast and Furious*. Launched five years after the Ford Mustang, and two years after the Chevrolet

③ A large choice of motors

Like other American muscle cars, the car was available with a wide range of motors, from the docile straight 6-cylinder 3.7 l through to the impressive 7.2 l V8 of the Charger R/T. Some just looked fast. And some actually were extremely fast.

④ A European flavour

The Dodge may be as American as apple pie, but it borrows quite a few styling cues from European sports cars of its time, including 'bumblebee stripes', hidden headlights at the front and the circular lights at the rear.

RYAN GOSLING
& CHEVROLET
CHEVELLE MALIBU SS 1973

Waiting game
As police sirens wail in the distance, the unnamed getaway driver (Ryan Gosling) waits in the car for five minutes. No more, no less.

*D*rive has it all. Finely honed nighttime cinematography and an exceptional sound track (especially 'Nightcall' the opening theme by French electro musician Kavinsky). And a peppering of references to Peter Yates's *Bullitt*, John Schlesinger's *The Day of The Locust*, or even the hippie vibe of Alejandro Jodorowsky (*El Topo)*. In 2011, Danish director Nicolas Winding Refn gave film buffs the world over a veritable classic among car movies, and was rewarded with 'Best Director' at the 64th Cannes Film Festival, as well as multiple nominations for Oscars and Césars. The film follows Ryan Gosling as the talented but taciturn driver who works in a garage by day, and is a getaway driver by night. The garage owner has an enviable collection of muscle cars from the 1960s and 70s, and Gosling, by day, drives a 1973 Chevrolet Chevelle Malibu SS, which he is still in the process of restoring (the paintwork is a matt grey undercoat). For his night driving, though, he uses a run-of-the-mill Chevrolet Impala (2006-2012), the most commonly sold car in the USA and so the most discreet car, too.

RYAN GOSLING & CHEVROLET CHEVELLE MALIBU SS 1973

An icon is born
Muscle car in matt grey,
satin jacket with a scorpion
embroidered on the back, and
chewing a toothpick: in *Drive*,
Gosling created a cult role.

Driving into cult status

The director succeeded in filming Los Angeles at
night with something reminiscent of the stylized
distance of Michael Mann (with *Miami Vice* or
Collateral, for example), while at the same time
bringing in a level of violence and suspense
worthy of Quentin Tarantino. Nicolas Winding
Refn had initially been considering Hugh
Jackman for the lead role but after a rather
inconclusive meeting with Ryan Gosling, Gosling
gave Refn a lift back from their meeting. Gosling
was driving and Refn was in the passenger seat.
According to Refn, it was only when he saw Ryan
Gosling driving, silent and concentrated, that he
knew he had found the right person for the role.
It was the drive itself that clinched it. The most
memorable part of the whole film is contained in
the five minutes during which the driver waits for
his accomplices to complete their armed robbery,
at the end of which time he will drive away, with
or without them. During these interminable
minutes, viewers of the film can feel the tension
mounting, as the driver stays put, listening to the
police sirens getting ever closer. It is a film that
has developed a cult following among film buffs
as much as with car enthusiasts. In many ways, it
is the antidote to the car chase film. The special
effects in the chases are not exceptional. And on
one occasion, when he needs to shake off his
pursuers, Gosling simply cuts the engine and
turns off the headlights, and waits for the police
to drive past. The film is undeniably Gosling's –
and with his satin jacket emblazoned with a silver
scorpion, and a toothpick in the corner of his
mouth, Gosling turned the driver into an icon.

The Italian Job
Michael Caine's gangster, helped by an assistant with a street map, reveals plans for the heist in this poster for the film. The Minis that made it all possible are not shown.

MICHAEL CAINE
& AUSTIN
MINI COOPER S MK II 1967

Michael Caine is like an antidote to James Bond. When he plays a spy in *The Ipcress Files* he travels by Tube or simply drives around in a van. But like Sean Connery and his successors, he is, nonetheless, the incarnation of British chic (see, for example Caine as Alfred Pennyworth, Batman's butler in the 2008 Batman movie *The Dark Knight*). Like the Bond characters, he was also a charmer of women (such as in *Alfie*, 1966), though in that film, he is driving a modest

Humber rather than an Aston. When, finally, in *The Italian Job*, in 1969, we do find him driving an Aston Martin (a 1960 DB4 Volante to be precise), this is not in the role of a spy working dutifully on behalf of Her Majesty's government, but as the leader of a powerful criminal gang. *The Italian Job* is a 'car film', but a paradoxical one. It begins with some shots of a magnificent Lamborghini Miura, which enters a tunnel, crashes and explodes, with the wreckage being dumped into a ravine shortly afterwards by a bulldozer. The Miura belonged to an English bank robber, Roger Beckermann, who wanted to organize an audacious heist in Turin.

The local mafia had other plans, and made this clear by crushing Beckermann's car with a bulldozer and then pushing it over the cliff.

A Mini adventure
Michael Caine and his gang
(and Mini Cooper S) prepare
for the heist of the century.

Later in the film, as Caine (playing criminal gang leader Croker) gets his own Turin heist plan underway, his Aston Martin meets a similar fate, but Caine and his gang talk their way out of trouble. With the luxury cars now out of action, enter the real star of the film: The Mini Cooper S. The genius plan was to create a huge traffic jam in Turin, allowing the bank robbers to escape in the three Minis, narrow enough to weave through the back alleys, arcades and even flights of stairs – and then to 'disappear' in the interior of a bus. It was a fabulous film-length advertisement for the Minis, which were seen jumping from rooftops, sliding around corners, and performing handbrake turns right under the noses of the Italian police who were trying to give chase. The Minis, of course, also finish up in a ravine. But they got the job done. And showed the world their extraordinary qualities.

AUSTIN
1967 MINI COOPER S MK II

ENGINE
Configuration **4-cylinder, in-line**
Capacity **1275 cc**
Fuel **Petrol**
Layout **Front engine, transverse**

TRANSMISSION
Gearbox **4-speed, manual**
Type **Front wheel drive**

DIMENSIONS
Length **3.05 m** / Width **1.41 m**
Height **1.35 m**
Weight **698 kg**

PERFORMANCE
Power **77 bhp**
Maximum speed **100 mph**

① Driven from the front

While most of the big-selling small cars of the 1950s and 60s were rear-engined (VW Beetle, Fiat 500, Renault 8), the Mini had a new architecture with its transverse engine mounted forward of the front axle. It was a game changer, with most small cars adopting the same layout in the decades that followed.

② A Mini epic

Between 1959 and 2000, more than five million Minis were sold across the world before it was replaced by the bigger and more spacious 'new' Mini. This model was created after BMW bought the brand, and retains many aspects of the characteristic styling of the classic model.

③ True Brit

Despite its diminutive size, the Mini's combination of curvy bodywork, round headlights, and its chrome grille called to mind the best of English sports car design from the 1950s – such as Triumph TR3, MGA and Austin-Healey.

④ A rally star

John Cooper, a technical genius of race preparation, made the most of the Mini's low centre of gravity, its exceptional handling, and light bodyweight to create an unbeatable racing machine – with the Mini Cooper becoming a three-times winner of the Monte-Carlo Rally.

ROBBERIES
AT THE WHEEL

'THIS HERE'S MISS BONNIE PARKER.
I'M CLYDE BARROW. WE ROB BANKS.'

Bank robberies and heist movies are a huge part of the American cinema tradition, with films like *Getaway* (1972) with Steve McQueen, *Straight Time* in 1978 with Dustin Hoffman, and Quentin Tarantino's *Reservoir Dogs* in 1992, to name just three. However, in all these films, the scenes of the getaway from the scene of the robbery are handled in just a few short scenes – often to avoid the expense of a full-on high-speed car chase sequence. And not all getaways use a car. We have also seen getaways by van (in Ben Affleck's *The Town*, 2010), by bus (*Dog Day Afternoon*, starring Al Pacino, 1975), on foot (*The Thomas Crown Affair*, starring Steve McQueen, 1968) or by underground train (*The Taking of*

Pelham 1 2 3, starring Denzel Washington and John Travolta, 2009). Even so, the getaway car remains the favoured way to make a quick exit. In *Heat* (1995) starring Robert De Niro and Al Pacino, we see a kind of robbery masterclass from director Michael Mann. While in *Gone in 60 Seconds*, in both the 1974 original and in the 2000 Hollywood remake with Nicolas Cage, it is cars that the gang are stealing: Ferrari, Porsche, Mustang. In some ways the heist movie is a descendant of the Western movie, with the car replacing the stagecoach, and the sub-machine gun replacing the six-shooter. And there are plenty of variants: vintage versions like *Bonnie and Clyde* in 1967, starring Warren Beatty and Faye Dunaway, or *Public Enemies*

in 2009, starring Johnny Depp and Marion Cotillard; there are European heists like *The Italian Job* in 1969, or *Mesrine* in 2008 with Vincent Cassel (driving a BMW); and Asian heist movies such as John Woo's *A Better Tomorrow* in 1986 with Chow Yun-Fat.

In most of these films, the driver is no longer just another member of the gang. Drive turned the getaway driver into the hero, but it was not the first film to do this. Along similar lines (a taciturn driver who ensures that the robbers escape from the police), you can see Ryan O'Neal and Isabelle Adjani in Walter Hill's *The Driver* (1978). This is a rare jewel of a film with its invigorating chase sequences in parking garages and through the empty reservoirs of Los Angeles.

BONNIE AND CLYDE (1967)
Ford Tudor Victoria 1934

THE DRIVER (1978)
Pontiac Trans Am 1977

THE DRIVER (1978)
Mercedes Benz 280 SE 1970

Bonnie and Clyde
Faye Dunaway and Warren Beatty take a break from robbing banks in front of their 1933 Plymouth De Luxe in Aurthur Penn's classic from 1967.

HEAT (1995)
Lincoln Town Car 1992

GONE IN 60 SECONDS (2000)
Mustang Shelby 1967 GT500

MESRINE (2008)
BMW 528i 1977

ARTISTS AT

THE WHEEL

4

THE BEATLES
& ROLLS ROYCE
1965 PHANTOM V 'GYPSY CARAVAN'

Fab Four
George Harrison and Paul
McCartney in tweeds, Ringo
Starr in black velvet, and John
Lennon in the camel jacket
celebrating passing his driving
test in a soft-top Triumph
Herald in 1965.

Pop stars in the 1960s were all about counter-culture. So you might think that luxury cars would not be the first thing on their mind. But these were a people who had made a fortune, and lived in an era when people wanted a taste of all of life's pleasures. So, along with the models and groupies they hung out with, and the crazy quantities of drugs and alcohol they consumed, there were also cars: lots of cars, and the bigger and more expensive, the better. Limousines, paradoxically, became the emblem of this counter-culture. Once a car exclusively for rich financiers, town hall bigwigs, or royalty, limousines became the mode of transport for this new pop aristocracy. Pete Townshend (The Who) and Keith Richards (The Rolling Stones) both owned Bentleys. Richards drove his to Morocco in 1968, along with the Stones's other guitarist Brian Jones and Jones's girlfriend, Anita Pallenberg.

Beatles car
All four Beatles owned a
mix of very different and
exotic luxury cars. But they
all drove Minis too.

Psychedelic
The second limo from
John Lennon's collection to
get a special paint job, this
1956 Bentley S1 was decorated
by fashion designer John Crittle,
and took on the appearance of a
giant butterfly.

Once in Morocco, Pallenberg left Jones for Richards, and Jones disappeared: this was the start of a hellish period in Jones's life which ended with his drowning, the following year, in his own swimming pool. Meanwhile, John Lennon managed to resolve the apparent contradiction between being a pacifist and revolutionary while at the same time driving around in priceless limos – by painting them in psychedelic colours – which is what he did with his Rolls Royce Phantom and his Bentley S1 (Janis Joplin did the same with her Porsche 356 cabriolet).

The Beatles became an icon of their era, and not just because of their music. The kinds of cars they drove were unlike any other band of their times. Predictably, the Fab Four drove around in Minis, another iconic symbol of the 1960s. But they also loved luxury and classic cars. So Lennon had his multi-colour Bentley. The genius drummer Ringo Starr had a Facel II, an imposing coupé powered by an American motor (a Chrysler Hemi 5.7 l), and one of the last genuine luxury cars to be made in France.

Understated
The Beatles posing alongside John Lennon's Rolls Royce Phantom V, with more discrete paintwork than some of his other cars.

'BABY, YOU CAN DRIVE MY CAR
YES, I'M GONNA BE A STAR
BABY YOU CAN DRIVE MY CAR
AND MAYBE I'LL LOVE YOU.'
'DRIVE MY CAR', THE BEATLES, 1965

Paul McCartney bought an Aston Martin DB6 (virtually identical to the Bond car). But it was guitarist George Harrison who was perhaps the biggest aficionado of fine cars: a Ferrari 275 GTB, followed by a yellow Dino 246 GTS (with removable top). And then there were the Harley-Davidsons, with Harrison getting involved with the Hells Angels in California, who had the (bad) idea of coming to London to stay with Harrison for the whole of 1968. He was also a friend of the triple World Champion Formula 1 racer Jackie Stewart, showing a taste for the thrills of motor racing that seemed in sharp contrast to Harrison's interest in zen-like calm and Eastern wisdom. Perhaps drawing on this kind of contradiction, Harrison produced his best solo album in 1971: *Living in a Material World*.

ROLLS ROYCE
1965 PHANTOM V
'GYPSY CARAVAN'

ENGINE
Configuration **8-cylinder, V8**
Capacity **6750 cc**
Fuel **Petrol**
Layout **Front engine, longitudinal**

TRANSMISSION
Gearbox **4-speed, automatic**
Drive type **Rear wheel drive**

DIMENSIONS
Length **6.00 m** / Width **2.00 m**
Height **1.80 m**
Weight **2500 kg**

PERFORMANCE
Power **170 bhp**
Maximum speed **103 mph**

① Rock – and Rolls

In 1967, John Lennon took his two-year-old Rolls Royce Phantom to a group of Dutch artists called The Fool for a paint job. They had already decorated some caravans in Lennon's garden.

② Romany style

The 'Beatles' Rolls' was inspired by the decoration of Romany caravans, and is very different from the psychedelic Bentley ordered by Lennon two years later (see page 102).

③ The last classics

With their flowing bodywork, the Rolls Royce Silver Cloud, Phantom (and Bentley S) can be seen as the last classics from the luxury carmaker. In 1965 Rolls Royce launched the Silver Shadow, which was very different: Americanised, angular and modern.

④ The limo of limos

Built between 1958 and 1991, the Phantom V and VI (with the Daimler DS420) were the last of the big English limousines. Queen Elizabeth II owned one – the Silver Jubilee Car – which was later used in the wedding of Kate and William. And the Sultan of Brunei placed an order for four more in the 1990s.

FRANK SINATRA
& FORD

1955 THUNDERBIRD

'TWO OR THREE CARS PARKED UNDER THE STARS
WINDING STREAM
MOON SHINING DOWN ON SOME LITTLE TOWN
AND WITH EACH BEAM, THE SAME OLD DREAM.'
'I THOUGHT ABOUT YOU' (1955)

In the 1950s, Frank Sinatra, along with his Rat Pack associates (including Dean Martin and Sammy Davis Jr.) invented a kind of classic masculine style. Decked out in impeccable navy suits, with silk square in the breast pocket and the obligatory Fedora, they moved easily from private jet to cabriolet and from studio to stage. Sinatra's life seemed to be constantly on show. In the afternoons, he would drive in his sports car to a film shoot, though not worrying too much about whatever it was the director wanted him to do. Then, he would hook up with his friends in one of the many new saunas, where they were regular customers. Time then for a few whiskies, before going on stage, slightly the worse for wear, to sing a few songs and swap jokes and wisecracks. Then, off to one of the nightclubs that Sinatra owned, surrounded by some of the world's most beautiful women. In the morning, they slept in the hotels or casinos of Miami, Palm Springs or Las Vegas, where the owners willingly gave shares to Sinatra to encourage him not go and stay elsewhere. And the following week, they would start all this again, in another city. A star by the age of 25, immensely rich, and an insatiable pleasure seeker, Frank Sinatra owned a lot of cars. He liked Chryslers, and drove several 1930s cabriolets from the US carmaker. By the end of the 1950s, he had also owned several Chrysler Ghias, a special edition model hand-built to order in Italy: elegant, if a little over the top.

A very good year
In 1955, Frank Sinatra appeared in Otto Preminger's *The Man with the Golden Arm*, as well as in *Guys and Dolls*, directed by Joseph Mankiewicz. He rewarded himself with a Ford Thunderbird. 'It was a very good year ...' as he used to sing.

Added to these, there were Lincoln, Cadillac, Rolls Royce and Jaguar. In 1966, Sinatra married Mia Farrow (*Rosemary's Baby*), who was 30 years younger than him (he was 51), and to celebrate the wedding he bought an impressive, deep orange Lamborghini Miura. But he had perhaps reached 'peak elegance' a decade earlier, in 1955, when he was photographed at the wheel of a Ford Thunderbird. He had just been through something of a slump in his career, and was making a comeback through movies, with *From Here To Eternity*, which won him an Oscar, followed by *The Man with the Golden Arm*. At the age of 40, he bought himself a Thunderbird, a drop-top that Ford had designed for a somewhat younger audience. But its sober elegance and sweeping lines, inspired by Italian sports cars, were a perfect match for Sinatra's tailored suits and classic elegance.

FORD
1955 THUNDERBIRD

ENGINE
Configuration **8-cylinder, V8**
Capacity **4.9 litres**
Fuel **Petrol**
Layout **Front engine, longitudinal**

TRANSMISSION
Gearbox **3-speed, manual or automatic**
Drive type **Rear wheel drive**

DIMENSIONS
Length **4.15 m** / Width **1.75 m**
Height **1.31 m**
Weight **1470 kg**

PERFORMANCE
Power **245 bhp**
Maximum speed **124 mph**

① The quiet American

While GM and Chrysler were battling to outdo each other with excessive chrome and futuristic styling, the Fords of the 1950s had about them a classic sense of calm. The lines were clean, with classic round headlights at the front, and reasonably sized (for the era) fins at the back.

② A direct line

Powerful (245 bhp), compact (just 4.15m long), straight, almost boxy, lines, the 'T-Bird' was designed to rival the European roadsters, which were selling well in the USA.

③ Strictly two-seater

Along with the Chevrolet Corvette in 1953, the Ford Thunderbird is the only mass-produced American two-seater cabriolet since the end of the Second World War.

ELVIS PRESLEY
& CADILLAC
1956 FLEETWOOD SERIES 60

'WHEN YOU LEFT YOU KNOW YOU TOLD
ME THAT SOMEDAY YOU'D BE RETURNIN'
IN A FANCY CAR ALL THE TOWN TO SEE, OH, YEAH
WELL, NOW EVERYONE IS WATCHING YOU,
YOU FINALLY HAD YOUR DREAM
YEAH, AND YOU'RE RIDIN' IN
A LONG BLACK LIMOUSINE.'
'LONG BLACK LIMOUSINE' (1969)

Elvis Presley, the King of Rock, had a kind of insatiable appetite for many things in life. Once he got started, it was difficult to stop – a tendency which accounted for drugs as much as it did for peanut butter or banana sandwiches. When it came to cars, it was a similar story.

He used his immense fortune to buy several new cars each year. Most of these can now be seen at Graceland, the Presley mansion in Memphis, Tennessee. A special annex is devoted to the collection, The Elvis Presley Automobile Museum, which contains a dozen Cadillacs from the 1950s to 1970s bought by Presley over the years through to his death in 1977, at the age of 42. There are European cars too, including cabriolets like the Mercedes 280 SL from the 1960s, a very rare BMW 507, and an MGA, as well as two Rolls Royces and a Ferrari 308 GT4 with spoked wheels for added bling. Even more flashy is Elvis's Stutz Blackhawk: one of a small limited edition of modern cars with vintage styling to be created in the 1970s by Virgil Exner (the man responsible for the most outrageous Chryslers of the 1950s).

With its unmissable headlights, protruding vertical grille, and lateral exhausts running along the bodywork, the Stutz was a car perfectly in

Viva Las Vegas
Elvis Presley with Ann-Margret
in the prototype race car that he
drives in *Viva Las Vegas* (1964).

step with a world inhabited by the King of Rock 'n'
Roll. Elvis bought the very first Blackhawk model
to be built, beating rival buyer Frank Sinatra who
wanted it just as badly. The museum also contains
several Harley-Davidsons, and various cars that
appeared in the Presley films, such as the pink jeep
from *Blue Hawaii*. Elvis appeared in around 30
films, including *Viva Las Vegas* (1964), where he
plays a racing driver. His film career also saw him
driving a Triumph TR3 and Ferrari 250 GT, as well
various prototype models. But among all these
varied cars that surrounded him over his career,
there was one to which he was particularly
attached: the iconic pink Cadillac. It was a plush
and luxurious four-door Fleetwood, with a white
roof and pristine white interior, which Elvis bought
in September 1956 for his mother, Gladys. The
story goes that from a very young age, Elvis used
to tell her: 'Mother, one day, I will buy you a
Cadillac ...' And after just three years of his singing
career, he was able to keep his promise. Sadly, his
mother did not live long enough to enjoy the car
– she died in 1958 at the age of 46, leaving her son
inconsolable and alone to battle with his bulimia,
his addictions – and to continue adding to his
collection of cars.

CADILLAC
1956 FLEETWOOD

ENGINE
Configuration **8-cylinder, V8**
Capacity **6 litres**
Fuel **Petrol**
Layout **Front engine, longitudinal**

TRANSMISSION
Gearbox **4-speed, Hydra-Matic automatic**
Drive type **Rear wheel drive**

DIMENSIONS
Length **5.74 m** / Width **2.00 m**
Height **1.57 m**
Weight **2300 kg**

PERFORMANCE
Power **285 bhp**
Maximum speed **123 mph**

① Fifties style

White wall tyres, wrap-around windscreen, and chrome everywhere: the Cadillac brought together every gimmick from American automotive style of the 1950s.

② Warheads up front

With bumpers shaped like warheads, fins at the rear, and (fake) air intakes down the sides, this is typical post-war US car design, drawing heavily on the styling of aircraft. Among the best examples are the models designed by Harley J Earl for GM's Cadillac range.

③ A pure Graceland car

Pink paintwork, white roof, a pristine interior ... Elvis Presley's Cadillac is typical of the preposterous styling of a prosperous America in the 1950s – as are most of the objects on show at Graceland.

④ Homage to a King

The Cadillac pictured is not Elvis's, but is practically identical to that of The King, and is the ultimate addition to the memorabilia of any serious fan.

Like a Rolling Stone

While less into their car collection than the Beatles, The Rolling Stones still got to drive some pretty beautiful cars, such as this Morgan Plus 8, seen here with a young Mick Jagger in Saint-Tropez in 1971.

Giulietta
The second *Crashed Car* exhibited in a gallery by the artist (the first was a Ferrari). Simply called *Giulietta*, eagle-eyed purists might want to point out that the car is actually an Alfa Romeo Alfetta GTV, rather than a Giulietta.

BERTRAND LAVIER
& CRASHED CARS

French artist Bertrand Lavier is not the most famous of contemporary artists, but he might just be the one to inspire the most envy among a certain gallery-going public. After all, he assembles a bunch of objects in the middle of a gallery, stacked one on top of the other. He smokes big cigars. And he drives a Ferrari. In short, he does everything possible to annoy traditional art lovers who think artists should paint pictures of scenery, live a bohemian life and ride around on a bicycle. Lavier has even said that he has been as much impressed by Enzo Ferrari as he has by Marcel Duchamp. And this 'enfant terrible' of the art world proves the point with his installations, which show a definite bias towards the world of cars – works such as *Dino*, consisting of the wreck of an accident-damaged Ferrari Dino 308 GT4, presented in the gallery as a work of art. The piece was sold for $250,000 in 2013, or *six times* the going price for a similar (undamaged) Dino of a similar age on the used car market. In 1993, he produced a similar work with a bashed up 1970s Alfa Romeo, simply named *Giulietta*. Lavier has picked up the idea of 'ready-made' objects (as did Marcel Duchamp) and run with it. He is perhaps also influenced by Andy Warhol's photography of car accidents from the 1960s (*Death and Disaster: Crash Series*). In 1998, one of his most complex pieces was based around a 308 GTS (as seen in the TV series *Magnum*). The car

has been painted by hand, using a crude paintbrush and thick paint, so the strokes of the brush are visible, even though the original colour has been retained. It is a work where the car itself is both the model and the finished artwork, at one and the same time. Lavier has also created the painting *Rosso Scuderia*, which superimposes the exact hues of Ferrari reds from 1993 to 2004, and from which it is apparent that a definitive Ferrari red does not really exist at all: it appears to have become paler as the years go on! Lavier is one of the heirs to the tradition of Anglo-Saxon pop art (Warhol, Lichtenstein ...) as well as the new French realism (César, Martial Raysse ...), for whom industrially-made objects are not the antithesis of works of art, but exciting creations in their own right, and with which the art world really does need to engage. César, for example, has shown numerous sculptures made from crushed or compressed cars, including Ferrari, and was himself once the owner of a 308. Bertrand Lavier is also a friend of Jean Todt (the boss of the Scuderia Ferrari racing team from 1993 to 2007, and himself a major art collector). Lavier's own private cars over the years have included a Ferrari 250 GTE (1960-1963), a 330 GT 2+2 (from 1964-1967), a Ferrari 400 (from 1976-1979), and, most recently, a Ferrari 360 Modena. It's also worth noting that none of his own Ferraris were red, a colour that seems to be reserved in his mind only for the team's racing colours ... and for Lavier's works of art.

CONTEMPORARY ARTISTS
& SPORTS CARS

Warhol car
In 1979, auctioneer and racing driver Hervé Poulain commissioned a BMW M1 to be re-painted by artist Andy Warhol for The 24 Hours of Le Mans.

Even though both Picasso and Salvador Dali owned a Rolls Royce, in common with many great artists and visionaries, they kept a discreet distance from the culture of the automobile. The same can be said for the architect, Le Corbusier. Even though he had devised a plan (on behalf of car manufacturer Voisin), to re-model Paris along the lines of New York, demolishing the whole of the centre of the city and replacing the buildings with skyscrapers lining a grid system of streets, he was in no shape or form a car enthusiast himself. At the same time, the Italian futurist movement was building a manifesto that put speed and modernity at the forefront. But neither Le Corbusier, nor the futurists, nor any of the other stars of radical thought of this time, had any serious leanings towards cars as objects of desire or indeed as art. Instead, you have to look back to the multi-talented Sonia Delaunay, creator of paintings and fabrics and decorative objects, who painted the bodywork of a number of cars (a Bugatti 35 in 1924; a Citroen 5CV in 1925) and some forty years later, a Matra 530 in 1967. But you have to wait until the 1960s before artists really started to get interested in cars, and to incorporate them into their work. Warhol used a series of photographs of cars involved in accidents, César put cars into a crusher, while the American hyperrealists, people like Richard Estes and Don Eddy, painted their chrome, the glass, and bodywork, creating infinite reflections. It was the French auctioneer Hervé Poulain who perhaps best illustrates this link between artists of this time and the cars that surrounded them. In 1975, he entered a BMW 3.0 CSL into The 24 Hours of Le Mans – a car that had its bodywork painted by Alexander Calder. In 1977, it was the turn of Roy Lichtenstein to make his mark on a high performance BMW race-car, and two years later, in 1979, a BMW M1 would

SONIA DELAUNAY
Bugatti 35 1924

SONIA DELAUNAY
Citroën 5CV 1925

SONIA DELAUNAY
Matra 530 1967

be decorated by none other than Andy Warhol. In the following years, BMW continued to commission 'art cars' from artists including David Hockney, Olafur Eliasson, and Jeff Koons. While these 'art cars' brought art, in a sense, onto the racetrack, other players were starting to bring cars themselves right into the art galleries. In 1993 in Paris, the Mexican artist Gabriel Orozco exhibited an extraordinary artwork based around the iconic Citroen DS: the car had been sliced in three from front to back, the middle section removed, and car welded back together, with the interior re-fitted with a single driver's seat in the front (and steering wheel and dashboard), and a single passenger seat behind. A decade later, the artist Erwin Wurm created incredible 'inflated' sculptures of cars from resin, with the vehicles appearing perhaps to have somehow swollen up in the sun. In a totally different direction, a Richard Prince installation takes a 1970 Dodge Challenger and places this on a podium, where it is accompanied by a (real life) young woman, scantily clad, polishing the bodywork with a soft cloth. The resulting scene evokes something about American automobile culture at its most grass roots level.

Cut and shut
In 1993, the Mexican artist Gabriel Orozco transformed a 1970 DS into a fantastical object that plays havoc with a viewer's perceptions. He sliced the original car in three from front to back, removed the middle section, and re-built the interior. From a side view, you would hardly notice.

GABRIEL OROZCO
Citroën DS 21 1970

ALEXANDER CALDER
BMW 3.0 CSL 1975

ANDY WARHOL
BMW M1 1979

FRANÇOISE SAGAN
& HER SPORTS CARS

JAGUAR XK120 CABRIOLET
1958 COUPE GREGOIRE SPORT
ASTON MARTIN DB2 CABRIOLET

In 1954, *Bonjour Tristesse* was published, and became an instant bestseller. Françoise Sagan, its author, a young woman just 19 years old, suddenly found herself with millions of francs. Her father, a company director, gave her some unusual advice about what to do with her new-found fortune: 'At your age, it's dangerous. So spend it!' Sagan followed his advice dutifully, buying herself a Jaguar XK120 and then heading off, with the roof down, to Saint-Tropez, where she was to spend the first of many summers. She drove 'barefoot, and with the wind in my hair',

'THIS SUMMER I WILL WRITE A BOOK,
IT WILL BE SUCCESSFUL, I WILL EARN A LOT OF
MONEY, AND I WILL BUY MYSELF A JAGUAR.'
FRANÇOISE SAGAN TO FLORENCE MALRAUX

creating a new kind of iconic figure, miles away from the stuffy idea of the 'gentleman driver' with his sturdy English leather boots and tweed motoring cap. In 1957, driving her Aston Martin DB2 cabriolet very fast on a country road near Fontainebleau, she lost control on a bend, the car rolled twice, and finished up in a wheat field. It took the emergency services more than half an hour to cut her out of the car, and a priest was rushed to the scene to administer last rites. In fact, she survived, spending weeks in a hospital bed, and developing a serious morphine addiction which went on to trouble her for the rest of her life (as documented in her book *Toxique*, in 1964). In a photograph taken after her recovery, she can be seen standing with a rueful smile, alongside the wreck of the car that nearly killed her like a kid caught in the act of some misdeed. (The distinguished French author and

Françoise Sagan in her 1958 Grégoire Sport coupé, one of the last of the French classic sports cars, and featuring bodywork by legendary coachbuilder Henri Chapron.

Nobel laureate François Mauriac described Sagan as a 'charming little monster'.)

Even so, the Aston accident did not dampen her enthusiasm for fast cars. She went on to drive plenty more, including a Buick Roadmaster Cabriolet, an E-Type Jaguar, an AC Cobra, a Lotus Super Seven and a splendid Ferrari 250 California, as well as several of the latest French sports cars, such as a Gordini V12 designed for Le Mans, and a Grégoire Sport. In her book *With Fondest Regards*, Françoise Sagan, experiencing acceleration and danger as a kind of drug, writes: 'Anyone who has never loved speed has never loved life – or, perhaps, has never loved anybody. 'In May 1968, when she went to the Odéon Theatre to meet with students and revolutionaries who had occupied the building, one of them shouted: 'So, Comrade Sagan, did you come here in your Ferrari?' She coolly shot back: 'It's not a Ferrari, comrade, it's a Maserati!' In the 1990s, as she reached her sixties, she drove a small, and rather beaten up Citroën AX Sport. But that didn't stop her from driving hard through the streets of Paris whenever possible.

WRITERS
AT THE WHEEL

There's a strong connection in many peoples' minds between writers and walking. Both Louis-Ferdinand Céline, in *Journey to the End of the Night*, and John Dos Passos in *Manhattan Transfer* write about walking endlessly through the city. If cars have to come into the story at all, then it's a beaten up Ford T Pickup that Steinbeck allows for the characters in *The Grapes of Wrath*, thrown onto the streets in the Great Depression, or the rickety old Chevrolets that Jack Kerouac gives to his band of drifters in *On The Road*. Even so, some famous writers have also been owners of some remarkable cars. Francis Scott Fitzgerald bought himself a Rolls Royce Silver Ghost with the earnings from his first novels – the same car, in fact, that *The Great Gatsby* himself drives in F Scott Fitzgerald's 1925 bestseller.

Oddly enough, in the film adaptations of the novel, the Silver Ghost is replaced with a later version of the Rolls in the 1973 version (with Robert Redford), and with a 1931 Duesenberg in the more recent Gatsby (with Leonardo DiCaprio) in 2012. Meanwhile, the celebrated French modernist author Paul Morand (*The Man In A Hurry*), who was married to an extremely rich Hungarian countess, built up an enviable collection of fine sports cars, including a pre-war Bugatti and an Alfa Romeo Zagato Coupé. But on the whole, cars have not had a particularly good image among the literati, and especially so in France. This may be due to two notable events. French literary giant Albert Camus, philosopher and author, who won the Nobel Prize for literature in 1957, was killed in a road accident: he was a

passenger in the powerful Facel Vega FV3B, driven by the publisher Michel Gallimard on 4 January 1960. And just two years later, another writer died on the roads – this time the 36-year-old author Roger Nimier in an accident on 28 September 1962 in an Aston Martin DB4.

In the US, where cars have always been more essential to daily life, if a writer were going to drive a car, that car would typically be a Volvo. Many novelists also took on jobs as teachers of Creative Writing on university campuses, and adopted a suitably writerly look, part of which was the tweed jacket and the obligatory Scandinavian estate car. There are of course plenty of exceptions to this rule. Hunter S. Thompson appears behind the wheel of a massive Cadillac coupé in *Fear and Loathing in*

FRANCIS SCOTT FITZGERALD
Rolls Royce Silver Ghost 1922

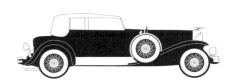

MICHEL GALLIMARD
(AND ALBERT CAMUS)
Facel Vega FV3B 1958

ROGER NIMIER
Aston Martin DB4 1962

Las Vegas, as seen in Terry Gilliam's film adaptation of the novel in 1998. In the celebrated novel by Joan Didion, *Play It As It Lays* (1970), there is a passage that describes the heroine driving a Chevrolet Corvette, foot to the floor, in the desert, in an attempt to forget her acting career, which has collapsed, and her crazy private life. In real life, Didion did in fact buy a 1968 Corvette Stingray, which seemed even more imposing when driven by this petite young woman. French novelist Michel Houellebecq made a scathing criticism of the Corvette in his novel *The Possibility of an Island*: '... the Chevrolet Corvette, with its uselessly and aggressively virile lines, with its absence of true mechanical nobility wedded to its overall modest price, is undoubtedly the one that corresponds best to the notion of *pimpmobile*.' Harsh, but maybe a grain of truth in that too.

Robert Redford and Rolls in *The Great Gatsby*, Jack Clayton's 1974 adaptation of the novel by F Scott Fitzgerald.

DRIVERS ON

PATRICK MACNEE **BENTLEY 4 ½ L 1927**

TOM SELLECK **FERRARI 308 GTS 1978**

PETER FALK **PEUGEOT 403 CABRIOLET 1960**

MIAMI VICE **FERRARI DAYTONA & TESTAROSSA**

JON HAMM **CADILLAC COUPE DE VILLE 1962**

DAVID DUCHOVNY **PORSCHE 911 CABRIOLET 1990**

SUV **ON TV**

PATRICK MCGOOHAN **LOTUS SUPER SEVEN S2 1967**

PATRICK MACNEE
& BENTLEY

4 ¹/₂ L 1927

'JOHN STEED: I'VE DRIVEN ACROSS THIS ROAD,
OOH, A HUNDRED TIMES DURING THE WAR.
EMMA PEEL: WELL, SINCE YOU KNOW IT SO WELL
IT'S REMARKABLE YOU COULDN'T STAY ON IT.'

THE AVENGERS, SERIES 4

The Avengers was a TV spy series dating from 1960, which started small and went on to gain a cult following. The initial seasons were filmed mainly in a studio in black and white, and the agent John Steed character had only a supporting role. But by the third season, the series was built on the sparky and witty relationship between its two central agents, one an 'establishment' man, and the other a feisty, smart and capable young woman, whose joint mission was to solve quirky mysteries in a mix of spy thriller and sci-fi drama.

Steed (played by Patrick Macnee) was first joined by Catherine Gale (Honor Blackman, who was to reappear in *Goldfinger* in 1963). In the fourth season in 1965, Diana Rigg took over from Blackman, playing the unforgettable Emma Peel. By then, the series had the budget to spend more time filming on location, and the show's characters began to be seen in cars which matched up with their fictional personas. So Steed drives a 1927 Bentley 4½, a huge racing machine which rival carmaker Ettore Bugatti labelled, bitterly, 'the fastest truck in the world'. In stark contrast, Emma Peel has a Lotus Elan, a diminutive roadster with a fibreglass body,

inspired by Lotus's recent success in Formula 1 (it was Champion in 1963 and 1965). The cars themselves perfectly illustrate the cultural gap between the English gentleman, impeccably dressed in his classic suit, and the young, capable woman, ready to take on anything – a notable first in TV series of the time. Emma Peel personified Swinging London in the 1960s, in her futuristic Pierre Cardin jumpsuits, and the title of the series in France captures the contrast between the two characters: 'Bowler Hat and Leather Boots'. In the sixth season of the show, in 1969, Linda Thorson took over from Diana Rigg, who, like Blackman, was to go on to play a Bond girl. Thorson's car was also a Lotus (an orange mid-engined Europa), but she later switched to an AC Frua: a bigger English cabriolet, designed in Italy and powered by an American engine. Steed's Bentley was in later series replaced by an even older vehicle, a Rolls Royce Silver Ghost from the early part of the 20th Century. Ironically,

Seeing a Ghost
Instead of the big Bentley, the
series producers chose an even
older Rolls Royce Silver Ghost
from 1910 for the press photos
to promote the fifth series of
The Avengers. The Rolls was to
become the new Steed-mobile
in the subsequent series.

'PATRICK MACNEE HATED
THESE ANTIQUE CARS, AND
STRUGGLED TO DRIVE THEM.'

Patrick Macnee hated these antique cars, and struggled to drive them.

So he was delighted when, in the two extra seasons filmed in 1976 and 1977 (*The New Avengers*), he was handed the keys to a new Jaguar – an XJ-C 12 Coupé, modified with a specially-prepared V12 engine and some dramatic (and slightly questionable) wing extensions. Purdey (Joanna Lumley), was also given a Jaguar, a pale yellow XJS coupé. A third agent joined the team, Mike Gambit (played by Gareth Hunt), twenty years younger than Steed and so better equipped to handle the more frenetic action sequences. Gambit's Avengers car was the angular wedge of the Triumph TR7, one of the most characteristic models of 1970s geometric car design. With a trio of agents, however, the series began to lose the wry and witty interplay between old and new, and male and female, which had been the secret of its success during the 1960s. The unsuccessful film version in 1998 (with Uma Thurman and Ralph Fiennes) was not enough to reignite interest in the series. And in a footnote to the film version, the Lotus Elan had to be swapped for an E-Type Jaguar, because the tall and elegant Thurman was not able to squeeze her six-foot frame into the cramped cockpit of the little roadster.

BENTLEY
1927 4¹/₂ L

ENGINE
Configuration **4-cylinder, in-line**
Capacity **4398 cc**
Fuel **Petrol**

DIMENSIONS
Length **4.38 m** / Width **1.74 m**
Height **1.12 m**
Weight **1330 kg**

① What Bentley?

So far as *The Avengers* producers were concerned, a Bentley was a Bentley. During the various episodes, John Steed was to drive various 4 ½ L, 3 L (1921-1928) and other Speed Six models (1926-1930). ·

② British Racing Green

Bentley was the first major racing team to adopt the team livery in British Racing Green, a colour which most other British motor racing teams were to copy, including Jaguar, Aston Martin and Lotus.

③ Destined to win

Bentley met with widespread success in motor racing during the 1920s. First, with the Bentley 3 L Sport, notably winners of The 24 Hours of Le Mans in 1924 and 1927. Then, with the 4 ½ L in 1928. And finally, in 1929 and 1930 with the Speed Six.

④ The original Bond car

The Bentley 4½ L (1927-1931) is James Bond's own personal car, as described in the novels by Ian Fleming, and also in the 1963 film, *From Russia With Love*.

Iconic
Big moustache, hairy chest,
Hawaiian shirt and sports
coupé. Thomas Magnum's style
set a trend in the 1980s.

TOM SELLECK
& FERRARI

308 GTS 1978

'IT IS NOT 'YOUR' FERRARI, THOMAS.
IT IS THE FERRARI OF MR ROBIN MASTERS.'

HIGGINS, IN *MAGNUM*

With the big moustache, hairy chest and exquisitely laid back manner, Tom Selleck seemed the ideal actor to become the new star of *Magnum P.I.*, CBS's new TV detective action series in 1980. The hero, Thomas Magnum, is a private detective, an ex-Navy Seal and Vietnam veteran, who is occasionally helped out by his former regimental comrades T.C. and Rick, helicopter pilot and gunner respectively. It would have been easy for CBS to make this a typical urban and violent action series. But Magnum was very different. This was the start of the 1980s, the decade of glamour and excess. So the series is set in Hawaii, (the biggest US marine base in the Pacific), and a location where Magnum's investigations take him to beaches inhabited by plenty of bikini-clad extras. Rick has a day job as the manager of an exclusive Honolulu beach club where Magnum spends much of his time when he is not working on investigations. And Magnum lives in the beachside villa of Robin Masters, a best-selling author who is always away. Magnum is supposed to take care of the security of the house (a task he takes fairly lightly) and in exchange, he gets to use the guest bungalow *and* drive around in Robin Masters' Ferrari (a red 308 GTS with Targa top, the descendant of Danny Wilde's famous Dino 246 GT in *The Persuaders!*). So, putting all this together, you end up with a tough guy former US marine, who likes to take life easy, living the life of the sexy jet-setter in Hawaii.

Once a soldier...
Despite his playboy lifestyle,
Thomas Magnum is a tough
former US marine who
knows how to handle a gun.

Plastic fantastic

The Ferrari seen in *Magnum, P.I.* is sometimes
replaced by a plastic-bodied replica, powered by
a Chevrolet Corvette engine, used mainly for
hard-driving action stunts. The replica was also
more generously sized, built to accommodate the
very tall Tom Selleck (1.92m) who struggled to
get into the extremely low-slung genuine Ferrari,
which had to be modified with seats bolted as far
back as they would go. Despite this sleight of
hand, the series did, of course, work wonders for
the reputation of the real 308, making it one of
the most recognisable Ferraris in the world.

It also played well for Selleck himself, who
became the first choice of Steven Spielberg and
George Lucas for the lead part in *Indiana Jones*.
Unfortunately, his contract with series creator
Donald P. Bellisario, who later went on to create
more blockbuster series including *Airwolf, JAG,*
and *NCIS*, prevented him from filming elsewhere.
Selleck was thus condemned to stay put by the
beach, under the warm Hawaiian sun, and drive
his fabulous Ferrari right through to the end of
the series in 1988. There are worse fates.

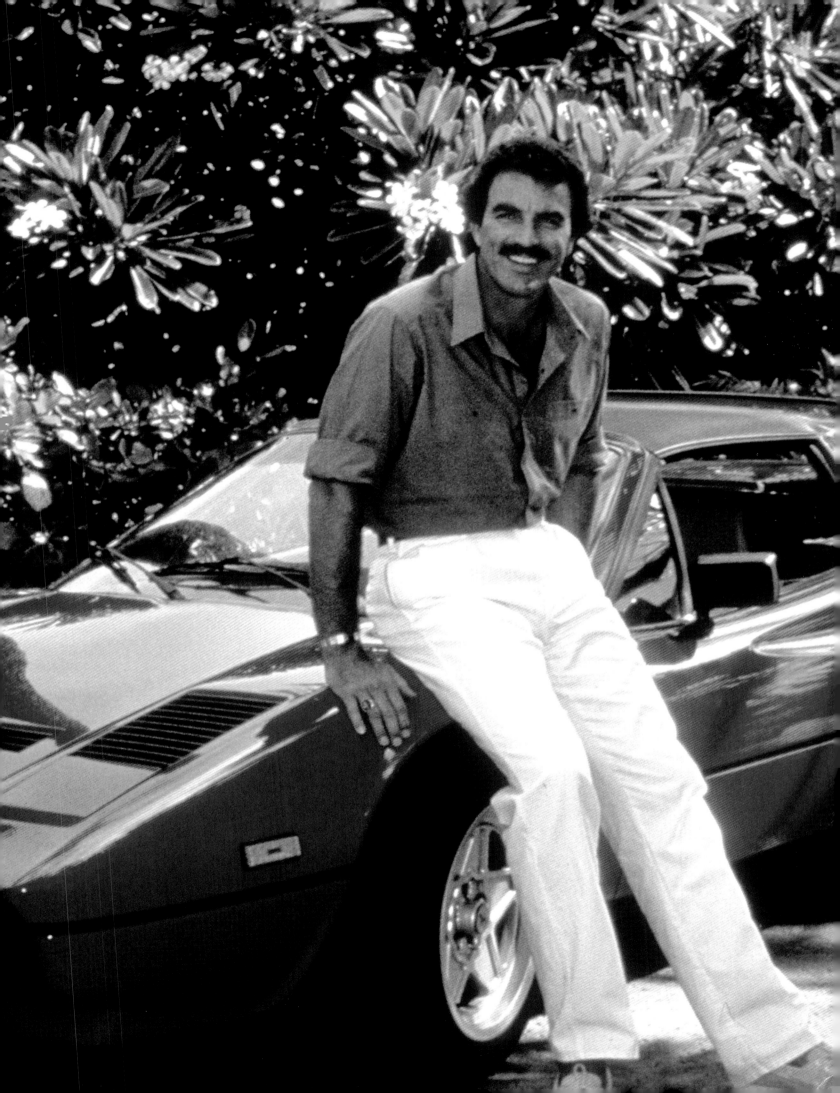

FERRARI
1978 308 GTS

ENGINE
Configuration **8-cylinder, V8**
Capacity **2926 cc**
Fuel **Petrol**

DIMENSIONS
Length **4.23 m** / Width **1.72 m**
Height **1.12 m**
Weight **1330 kg**

① Built for the sun

The 308 came in two versions. The GTB, with a fixed hard top. And the GTS with a removable Targa top, which is the car used by Thomas Magnum.

② The first V8

Building on the architecture of the Dino 246 GT, the 308 is the first Ferrari equipped with a V8 engine. Styled by Pininfarina, as are most Ferraris, the body was built in polyester composites from 1975 to 1977, after which it

③ Changing with the seasons

Magnum upgraded Ferrari models several times during the series. He started with the 308 GTS in 1978, then moved on to a GTSi in 1980 (with fuel injection) and finally a 308 GTSi Quattrovalvole (with four valves

④ Vanity plates

Magnum's Ferrari is also famous for its vanity number plate: 'Robin 1'. Its owner, the writer Robin Masters, also owned an Audi 200 with the plate 'Robin 2'.

PETER FALK
& PEUGEOT
403 CABRIOLET 1960

Old school
Among the Hollywood stars and wealthy of Beverly Hills, Columbo stands out in his ancient and beaten-up Peugeot 403 (see especially the state of those front headlights).

Peter Falk, who plays Lieutenant Columbo, was one of the go-to actors for pioneering independent film director John Cassavetes (*Husbands, A Woman Under The Influence* ...), and was a character actor more used to New York's original and independent film scene, rather than that of the Hollywood studios producing major TV series. So when *Columbo* was being made, Falk was quick to add essential details that made the part his own: it was his idea that the detective inspector should be more than a little shabby in appearance: unkempt hair, messed up necktie, and the famously grubby raincoat. In the same vein, he selected, from the studio's vast collection of cars, a Peugeot 403 cabriolet that had been gathering dust there for more than ten years. It was a model that had never been on sale in the USA, and what it was doing in the parking garage, nobody seemed to know. (Only later did the French actor Roger Pierre confirm that it was in fact his own private car!). The Columbo character was complete and this run-down aspect of the detective – and his car – was set in sharp contrast against his fictional adversaries. The murderers he tries to bring to justice are, for the most part, drawn from the wealthy middle classes (surgeons, film producers, investors, bankers), played by guest stars from cinema and TV: Martin Landau (*Mission: Impossible*), Patrick McGoohan (*The Prisoner*), Faye Dunaway (*Bonnie*

Coast to coast
Peter Falk moved straight from the independent movie scene in New York, where he was working with director John Cassavetes, to the very Californian setting of NBC – without really changing his style. This suited his character. Columbo, after all, was a former New York detective, transplanted to the West Coast.

Fifties style
Floral skirts and a picnic in the countryside: an advertisement from the 1950s for the Peugeot 403. Manufactured from 1955 to 1966, it became one of the symbols of France during three prosperous post-war decades.

'MIKE ALEXANDER: I ONLY WORK ON FOREIGN CARS. LIEUTENANT COLUMBO: OH, IT'S A FOREIGN CAR. MIKE ALEXANDER: OH, I KNOW, BUT ... THERE ARE LIMITS, MATE, YOU KNOW?'

and Clyde), Janet Leigh (*Psycho*). They inhabit huge mansions in Beverly Hills or Bel Air, and drive every luxury car imaginable (including E-Type Jaguar, Bentley Continental, Mercedes SLC, Citroën SM).

His unassuming manner and his beat-up old car generally led his suspects to make the grave error of underestimating his skills, and answering his seemingly idiotic questions without thinking. It is ironic that his Peugeot, chosen as an understatement, rapidly became an automotive icon. On today's classic car market, the 403 cabriolet will typically fetch more than double the price of its successor, the Pininfarina-styled 404. The series was shown across the world between 1968 and 1978, before being re-launched, still with the original car, between 1989 and 2003. But when, finally, the series producers wanted to replace the worn-out old Peugeot with a newer model in better condition, Peugeot flatly refused to sell them one, worried that its use in the TV series would actually create a bad image for the brand. The studio workshops therefore had to cut the roof off two successive 403s to create 'fake' cabriolets. It is highly likely that the success of Columbo encouraged producers of other American TV action series to provide lead characters with more unusual cars in subsequent shows – as seen in *Magnum P.I.* for example, or *Miami Vice*.

PEUGEOT
1960 403 CABRIOLET

ENGINE
Configuration **4-cylinder, in-line**
Capacity **1468 cc**
Fuel **Petrol**
Layout **Front engine, longitudinal**

TRANSMISSION
Gearbox **4-speed, manual**
Drive type **Rear wheel drive**

DIMENSIONS
Length **4.47 m** / Width **1.67 m**
Height **1.51 m**
Weight **1230 kg**

PERFORMANCE
Power **58 bhp**
Maximum speed **100 mph**

① **One in 2,043**

More than 1.2 million Peugeot 403 models were built in total, but of these, only 2,043 were in

② **Cabriolets for the people**

Peugeot is the only French carmaker to systematically build a cabriolet version for each of its

③ **Winning lines**

With its round headlights and slab-sided 'ponton' styling, the 403 looked similar to many

Eighties style
Designer suits,
Wayfarer shades,
and drop-top Ferrari:
the most stylish
cops on TV.

MIAMI VICE
& FERRARI
DAYTONA AND TESTAROSSA

'BRENDA: HOW DO YOU GO FROM
THIS TRANQUILITY TO THAT VIOLENCE?
SONNY CROCKETT: I USUALLY TAKE THE FERRARI.'
MIAMI VICE (SEASON 1)

Here's the situation: There are two playboys, one white (Sonny Crockett, played by Don Johnson) and one black (Ricardo Tubbs, played by Philip Michael Thomas) who drive an exclusive Ferrari Daytona Spyder (and occasionally, a 1964 Cadillac Coupé De Ville convertible). They are dressed in expensive Italian designer suits in pastel colours. And what's more, Sonny lives on a yacht (a 13m Endeavour 42) that he shares with a pet alligator, and also owns a speedboat (an extremely powerful Wellcraft Scarab 38). And funding this lavish lifestyle: drug dealing. But all is not as it seems, because the two men are in fact undercover Miami cops, working on taking down

the city's drug barons. The series was launched in 1984, and the idea of portraying cops who lived a life of luxury was very much in step with the bling culture of the eighties. What's more, the Ferrari in the early series was actually a fiberglass replica with a Chevrolet Corvette underneath – and the fake Ferrari matched perfectly the fake lifestyle created for the two cops, and even the location itself: some of the Art Deco houses overlooking Miami Beach were repainted in pastel colours just for the filming.

The series was such a success, however, that the owners of other beachfront homes started to repaint them in similar colours, hoping to get their own properties pictured on TV, and the series became a major impetus in the rebirth of

Undercover?
A cabriolet is not always ideal for surveillance ops under the heat of the Miami sun. Happily, in 1986, the two cops were able to swap their drop-top Daytona for a Testarossa.

Miami as a beach resort. Meanwhile in Italy, Enzo Ferrari was distinctly unimpressed by the studio's use of fake Ferraris. His response, however, was to send the production team two 1986 Testarossas to use instead. Unfortunately the cars were black, so had to be re-sprayed white to make them suitable for filming at night. The producers also created yet another Ferrari replica for stunt sequences, this time based on a De Tomaso Pantera and powered by a robust Ford V8, but had to undertake to Ferrari to destroy the vehicle at the end of the series. The relationship between Ferrari and *Miami Vice* creator and executive producer Michael Mann remained strong through this time and beyond: three decades later, with Mann a celebrated film director (*Heat*, *Collateral*, *Public Enemies* ...) he announced plans to make an Enzo Ferrari biopic.

FERRARI
1986 TESTAROSSA

ENGINE
Configuration **12-cylinder, V12**
Capacity **4943 cc**
Fuel **Petrol**
Layout **Mid-engine, longitudinal**

TRANSMISSION
Gearbox **5-speed, manual**
Drive type **Rear wheel drive**

DIMENSIONS
Length **4.48 m** / Width **1.98 m**
Height **1.13 m**
Weight **1506 kg**

PERFORMANCE
Power **390 bhp**
Maximum speed **180 mph**

① Mirror image

Aiming to give the driver better visibility behind the car's wide rear end, stylists at Pininfarina came up with a single high-level door mirror mounted on the driver's side on twin aerodynamic support arms. You'll either love it or hate it. Most buyers wanted a second one for safer lane-changing.

② A real head turner

With the long side strakes running into the air scoops, the Testarossa has a breathtaking silhouette: refined at the front, and of massive girth at the back, all the while preserving the signature sculpted lines typical of Pininfarina's studio.

③ Egg slicer style

The side scoops are 'straked', designed to guide air straight into the twin side-mounted radiators. This became a styling trend widely copied, (and not just on cars), and also, notably adopted by Ferrari's Italian arch-rival Lamborghini on its 25th Anniversary model of the Countach.

④ Revolutionary rear view

The Testarossa dropped the paired circular tail light arrangement that had become a styling feature for the previous decade, and instead used a full-width satin black louvre that covered the rectangular light units.

California dream
When Don Draper goes on business to California, he rents a 1964 Imperial Crown Victory, an imposing four-door cabriolet, and the ultimate status symbol of the time.

JON HAMM
& CADILLAC
COUPE DE VILLE 1962

'EVERY TIME WE GET A CAR, THIS AGENCY TURNS INTO A WHOREHOUSE.'

DON DRAPER (JON HAMM) IN *MAD MEN*.

Period dramas often say as much about the times in which they were made, as about the era in which they are set. Cars take little more than a supporting role in *Mad Men* (2007-2015), and were probably much less important in the universe of screenwriter Matthew Weiner than in the America of the 1960s. During the show's first seasons, we see John Draper, the enigmatic and charismatic advertising man played by John Hamm, travelling by train from the suburbs. When he is not spending the night with one of his mistresses, he commutes each morning from Westchester, north of New York City, to his office in Madison Avenue, at the heart of Manhattan. His wife, Betty Draper, one of the few members of the cast who is seen driving a car, has a 1957 Ford Country Sedan, a big two-tone estate, in which she carries her children and all her preoccupations as an unhappy suburban housewife. Later in the series, Draper owns a silver 1962 Cadillac De Ville with a white roof – a gigantic, verging on flabby, two-door model more

than 5.6m in length. These luxury models from Cadillac, Buick, Chrysler and Lincoln were of course designed as pure status symbols. In the series, Don Draper is seen driving his fairly infrequently, and 'makes do' with the same car over several seasons of the drama, rather than changing cars each year, as he could well afford to do.

That said, as the series progressed, cars took on a more and more important role. The agency expanded into Los Angeles, where Draper rents a superb 1964 Imperial Crown Victory during his trip. Later, when his new wife Megan moves in to pursue her acting career, Draper buys her an Austin Healey 3000 MKII, a small English roadster that was bourgeois, bohemian and Californian all at the same time. But the most serious connection between *Mad Men* and American car culture was made when the agency won the Chevrolet account – and took part in the launch campaign for the Camaro, a sports coupé to rival the Mustang.

JON HAMM & CADILLAC COUPE DE VILLE 1962

L.A. Woman
A younger wife, an English cabriolet (Austin Healey 3000 MKII) and a house in the Hollywood Hills. The new life of Don Draper (John Hamm) in the final seasons of *Mad Men*?

The series could then take a look at two very different cultures: on the one hand, the urbane and sophisticated New York advertising creatives; and on the other, the more rugged and rural marketing team from the car industry. Ken Cosgrove, one of the agency's account men, paid the price when he lost an eye in an accident during a drunken hunting escapade with his clients. It's almost as if Don Draper, the former pedestrian, had finally been caught up in the automotive spirit of the United States. And with bases in Los Angeles, New York and Detroit, the series could explore the contrasting reactions of America in the face of the huge changes experienced during the 1960s – and most notably in its relationship with the car.

160

DAVID DUCHOVNY
& PORSCHE
911 CABRIOLET 1990

Porschification
The Porsche cabriolet, blue sky, pretty girls, and palm trees ... the idea of pleasure, *Californication* style.

There are certain things that a man over 30 is supposed to stop doing, like wearing a leather jacket and t-shirt, chain smoking, or driving around in a Porsche cabriolet (assuming he had the opportunity to do so previously). And that's what's likeable about Hank Moody in the series *Californication*, because from one episode to the next, he does all three. The actor who plays Moody, David Duchovny, was 47 when the first episode was filmed in 2007, and the role allowed him to make a total break with his previous screen persona – ten years portraying FBI agent Fox Mulder in *The X-Files*. In *Californication*, he can re-invent himself in the role of the alcoholic writer, a compulsive and desperate playboy (and borderline sex addict) who heads to Hollywood to try his luck as a screenwriter. The character of Hank Moody is the archetype of the epic loser that we love on screen – and steer clear of in real life.

His Porsche is a symbol both of his freedom, and also of his immaturity. He is unable to

Breakdown
The car is not working, and
nor is the hair ... Moody's
Californian dream heads for
midlife crisis.

'I'VE SPENT MY WHOLE LIFE
PRACTICING ZEN AND THE ART OF
WHO GIVES A F***? AND NOW I
JUST WANT TO GET IN THE
PORSCHE AND DRIVE.'
DAVID DUCHOVNY IN *CALIFORNICATION* (SEASON 4, EPISODE 10)

change, to give it up, to move on to the next
phase of his life. As long as he drives this German
sports car, he is not totally out of the game. The
exact model doesn't matter – as long as it is a
convertible. At the start of the series, Moody is
driving a 15-year-old Porsche 911, with a smashed
up light. In some of the promotional pictures, he
is pictured in the 356 Speedster of James Dean
fame. During the run of seven seasons, he is seen
buying a brand new 911, only for it to be stolen.
Then he borrows a Porsche from his agent, who,
recently divorced, has chosen the same car to
give himself a younger image. These various cars
have just one thing in common: black paintwork,
and beige leather interior. It is as if Moody is
constantly surrounded by starkly opposing
choices which are as black-and-white as his car
but impossible for him to reconcile: the need to
choose between his ex-wife and all the other
women in his life; between writing literature and
writing for the film industry; between work, and
pleasure. There are no car chases or even long
journeys by car in *Californication*. Instead, the car
is above all else, and almost uniquely, an
extension of its owner's ego. But isn't this often
the case in life?

SUV
ON TV

'HOW MANY TIMES I'VE TOLD YOU IT'S AN SUV: WATCH WHERE YOU PARK OFF ROAD – THE CATALYTIC CONVERTER AND THE DRY VEGETATION.'

TONY SOPRANO (SERIES 6)

With TV series being mostly produced in the USA, they are in some ways a global extension of American automobile culture. Since the 2000s, the SUVs – Sport Utility Vehicles, or big luxurious 4x4s – have largely replaced the luxury saloon car of the wealthy, and they have pride of place in most TV dramas. In *The Sopranos* (1999-2007), Tony Soprano drives a Chevrolet Suburban, which he later replaces with an even bigger Cadillac Escalade. Kiefer Sutherland's Jack Bauer is also driving a Suburban in *24* before opting for a Ford Expedition. Meanwhile in *CSI: Miami*, the forensic team drives a Hummer H2, the enormous military 4x4 converted into a super-luxurious

SUV: a great promotion for Hummer, but maybe not the most affordable vehicle for a police forensic team. More believably, perhaps, in *Homeland*, Brody, the US marine suspected of being a terrorist, owns a more everyday Chevrolet Tahoe – the vehicle which ends up exploding at the CIA headquarters. If any further proof was needed of the supremacy of the SUV in contemporary US fiction, in *House of Cards*, Frank Underwood, despite his voracious thirst for power, remains loyal to his GMC Yukon. This is the same model as the Chevrolet Suburban, but carries the badge of General Motors' trucks division – a means for the astute Underwood to show just

---

THE SOPRANOS (1999-2007)
Cadillac Escalade

THE SOPRANOS (1999-2007)
Chevrolet Suburban

24 (2001-2010)
Ford Expedition

how close he is to the American people. Once installed as President of the United States, he of course uses the Cadillac limousine like all his predecessors. As for many of the British dramas, the SUVs – or 4x4s – are typically Range Rover or Land Rover (*Spooks*, or *MI-5*) , which is also the case with some of the Scandinavian crime series (like *The Killing*), though there are plenty of Volvos in those too, including the SUV variants. These days, the demands for realism in our contemporary TV series tends to make them less exciting than, say, 30 years ago, in terms of the cars that are featured – but with just a few notable exceptions. In the black comedy *Six Feet Under*, viewers are treated to a macabre procession of vintage Cadillac hearses spanning decades; and in *Nip/Tuck*, you can only laugh at the choice of car of plastic surgeon Dr Christian Troy: a bright orange Lamborghini Gallardo cabriolet. We are of course a long way from the profusion of exceptional cars seen in the 1970s and 1980s, and it's no doubt because the whole era has moved on. In 2009, when NBC attempted to re-launch *Knight Rider*, they pensioned off David Hasselhoff's Pontiac Firebird Trans Am as the intelligent car 'KITT', and brought in a modern day Ford Mustang Shelby GT500 KR in its place. With low audience figures, the series was dropped after the first season. Maybe if KITT had been an SUV, the outcome may have been different.

CSI : MIAMI (2002-2012)
Hummer H2

HOMELAND (2010-...)
Chevrolet Tahoe

HOUSE OF CARDS (2013-...)
GMC Yucon

PATRICK MCGOOHAN
& LOTUS

SUPER SEVEN S2 1967

'I KNOW EVERY NUT AND BOLT AND COG – I BUILT IT WITH MY OWN HANDS!'

THE PRISONER, EPISODE 7

In the TV series *The Prisoner*, we find the main character, played by Patrick McGoohan, living in a beachside holiday village full of strange baroque style ornamental buildings, in what could be taken for southern Italy. The inhabitants, who look like smartly dressed 1960s British holidaymakers, drive around – at no more than 10 mph – in yellow and white Mini Moke beach buggies. The man has been aBRucted, and cannot escape. In this place, his captors tell him, he is known as 'Number 6'. He is not happy about it: 'I am not a number, I am a free man,' he protests. In a previous life, he had been a spy (viewers recognized the actor from the preceding TV series *Danger Man*), but he quit his job and was immediately kidnapped and taken to this village, where he remains a prisoner – because he will not reveal the information his captors demand.

This backstory is brilliantly captured in the introductory sequence to each episode, where Patrick McGoohan, who plays Number 6, is seen briefly driving a Lotus Super Seven through the streets of London. This Lotus was the quintessential English roadster, which gave drivers a taste of a Formula 1 car adapted for the road: bodywork in aluminium, a powerful Ford Cosworth engine, and a stripped-down approach, with nothing included that was not essential. The Seven was even available as a kit, and the entire car weighed just 500kg, perfectly illustrating the philosophy of Lotus's founder Colin Chapman: 'Light is right'. This maxim, and Chapman's genius, led Lotus to win seven F1 world championships between 1963 and 1978. Like the Lotus Elan driven by Diana Rigg in *The Avengers*, the appearance of the Lotus Super Seven in *The Prisoner* did much for its commercial success, even though it was on screen for several seconds only at the start of each episode, and scarcely longer in Episode 9 (when Number 6 manages to escape to London, before being recaptured and returned to the village). And it became the symbol of the man's lost liberty. *The Prisoner* had an enormous popular success throughout its first season in 1967-1968.

But the series climaxed on a surreal and

169

PATRICK MCGOOHAN & LOTUS SUPER SEVEN S2 1967

Lotus Super Seven
Seen in the opening sequence of every episode of *The Prisoner*, the Super Seven quickly gained cult status.

Mini Moke
In the fourth episode, 'Number 6' mounts an election campaign from the back of a Mini Moke beach buggy – the only cars permitted in the village.

psychedelic note that raised more questions than it answered, and disappointed and confused viewers who were hoping for a more classic wrap-up to the whole mysterious saga (though it ensured a cult following over the decades that followed). The series was not re-commissioned. McGoohan, who was writer, actor, and producer on some of the episodes, returned to America to continue working in film and TV, (and notably turned down the role of James Bond). He directed five episodes of *Columbo* (he was a friend of Peter Falk) and won two Emmys for his work with the series. In the *Columbo* episode *Identity Crisis* in 1975, he plays a spy driving a sea-green Citroen SM coupé – perhaps bringing back some memories from times past. He also reprised his role as Number 6 in an episode of *The Simpsons* in 2000.

LOTUS
1967 SUPER SEVEN S2

ENGINE
Configuration **4-cylinder, in-line**
Capacity **1350cc**
Fuel **Petrol**
Layout **Front engine, longitudinal**

TRANSMISSION
Gearbox **5-speed, manual**
Drive type **Rear wheel drive**

DIMENSIONS
Length **3.38 m** / Width **1.57 m**
Height **1.00 m**
Weight **495 kg**

PERFORMANCE
Power **85 bhp**
Maximum speed **100 mph**

① Light fantastic

The Lotus uses a very lightweight steel spaceframe, with the Ford engine mounted at the front and driving the rear wheels. Bodywork was in cheap, flat, aluminium panels, though the nose cone and wheel arches were later supplied in fibreglass.

② Six decades of Seven

When Lotus wanted to move on from 'kit cars' 1972, the UK's sole Lotus dealer Caterham bought the license to take over the Seven business, selling kits and completed cars. So between Lotus and Caterham, the model has been running for six decades.

③ Stripped down

The Lotus Seven is Spartan: weighing less than 500kg, standing just one metre high, a tight squeeze for two people, and no room for luggage, it is the ultimate stripped down sports car.

④ Build Your Own

With its Ford engine and Triumph suspension, the Lotus Seven was a perfect kit car, designed to be built by the customer, and using cheaply-sourced parts from mass-produced vehicles. They were a big hit in the UK, where the tax

FAMOUS DU

CLINT EASTWOOD FORD GRAN TORINO 1973

BRIGITTE BARDOT ALFA ROMEO 2600 SPIDER 1962

JEAN-LUC GODARD ALFA-MALE

MICHAEL J. FOX DELOREAN DMC-12 1983

BARRY NEWMAN DODGE CHALLENGER

THE ROAD MOVIE BOX OFFICE WINNERS

JEFF BRIDGES TUCKER TORPEDO SEDAN 1948

ROBERT DE NIRO CHECKER MARATHON 1975

TAXI BLUES

BATMAN & BATMOBILE

CLINT EASTWOOD
& FORD
GRAN TORINO 1973

The Gran Torino is an extremely large and fairly sporty-looking coupé, built between 1972 and 1976. It lived in the shadow of the more famous Ford coupés of its time – the Mustang and the Thunderbird. But the Gran Torino got a lucky break in Hollywood, where it was to become the iconic red and white coupé of David Starsky in the police crime series *Starsky and Hutch*, thanks in large part to George Barris, the legendary Hollywood car customiser. Barris was famous for building the Batmobile in the 1960s *Batman* series, as well as some of the KITT cars in *Knight Rider*, and it was his idea to add the iconic white band and various sports accessories to the car. (Ford even went on to build a limited edition of 1,000 'Starsky' models). The series was a game-changer, partly because of its level of violence, (which seems fairly benign by today's standards), but also because Paul Michael Glaser (Starsky) and David Soul (Hutch) were wearing jeans and trainers, and gleefully traded insults and banter, making a break with the much more formal portrayal of law enforcement in the US police dramas of their time. William Blinn, the series creator, first intended them to be driving in a green Chevrolet Camaro. But Aaron Spelling, the producer, had some prior arrangements with Ford. The choice was to have been a Mustang, but Ford then insisted on supplying a new Gran Torino for the film, a brand that it wanted to promote at the time.

Fast forward thirty years to 2008. In *Gran Torino*, the film directed by and starring Clint Eastwood, Eastwood's lead character Walt Kowalski is a former Ford factory worker and owner of a prized dark green 1973 Gran Torino (the model preceding the *Starsky and Hutch* car). The name Kowalski is shared with the lead character in the frenetic 1971 road movie *Vanishing Point*, see page 195) but in *Gran Torino*, the car spends much of its time locked in Kowalski's garage. Eastwood had a keen appreciation of automobile culture (even if he generally drove Mercedes or Ferrari), and the choice of Gran Torino was deliberate: the big and somewhat downmarket coupé stands as a symbol of a lost American era – when petrol was cheap, before the price rises and economic hardships of the 1970s. The year after Eastwood's film came out, a green Gran Torino is again seen in cinemas, this time in *Fast and Furious 4* (2009) and driven by the drug dealers. We can't draw too many conclusions from this choice, as the *Fast and Furious* production team managed to use pretty much every sports model ever built in Detroit in the course of the various movies. What this does show, though, is that a fairly insignificant car (which the Gran Torino undoubtedly was) can quickly gain iconic status from a series of chance (movie) events.

FORD
1973 GRAN TORINO

ENGINE
Configuration **8-cylinder, V8**
Capacity **7536 cc**
Fuel **Petrol**
Layout **Front engine, longitudinal**

TRANSMISSION
Gearbox **4-speed manual or 3-speed automatic**
Drive type **Rear wheel drive**

DIMENSIONS
Length **5.40 m** / Width **2.08 m**
Height **1.33 m**
Weight **1850 kg**

PERFORMANCE
Power **375 bhp**
Maximum speed **130 mph**

① Torino for the people

The Torino is basically a very ordinary mid-priced saloon car. But it came in various versions, including a two-door fastback (Sport Roof) and coupé (Sport Top), and was also available with a bigger engine: so it became the Gran Torino Sport, the car chosen by Eastwood in his film.

② Coke bottle styling

The rounded and softened lines of the 1973 Gran Torino are typical of the last generation of cars to be designed before the petrol crisis of the 1970s, and are commonly likened to the contours of the traditional bottle of coke. In the years that followed, cars became more boxy in shape, and above all a lot smaller.

③ Built for tail slides

With suspension equivalent to that of European cars from two decades before (i.e. from the 1950s, with a rigid rear axle with leaf spring suspension) the Gran Torino had a rather approximate road-holding, which explains the entertaining tail slides during the car chases in *Starsky and Hutch*.

④ Bigger than it looks

The Gran Torino was enormous – 5.4 m long, a good 70 cm longer than the Mustang driven by McQueen in *Bullitt*. From a distance, the Gran Torino looks like a US sports coupé, but it actually has the length of a big European limousine.

Starsky and Hutch
David Soul and Paul Michael Glaser in *Starsky and Hutch* (1975-1979). With their laid-back style, constant banter and Starsky's trademark red and white 1975 Gran Torino, the series revolutionised American police dramas.

BRIGITTE BARDOT
& ALFA ROMEO
2600 SPIDER 1962

Starlet
From the 1950s, the young Bardot seemed to develop a liking for Alfa Romeo. Here, she is with a racing version from the 1930s while filming *Le Mépris*.

Brigitte Bardot became the incarnation of women's freedom and rights. With the film *...And God Created Woman* in 1956, she contributed (along with her friend the author Françoise Sagan) to the success of the beach resort of Saint-Tropez. In the film, there is a memorable scene in which Bardot, as Juliete Hardy, and the character Antoine Tardieu (Christian Marquand) share a passionate embrace across the boot of a magnificent Lancia Aurelia Spider. This car, owned by the billionaire Eric Carradine, (played by Curd Jürgens) is symbolic of the rapid transformation of this little fishing port into a playground for the jet set – of which both Brigitte Bardot and Françoise Sagan were an integral part. Bardot lived there like a local: to make the journey between La Madrague, her secluded house by the sea, and the village itself, she drove in a Floride, a popular and elegant cabriolet made by Renault. Later, she drove a Mini Moke, a kind of micro-jeep based on the Austin Mini. In Paris at the start of the 1970s, she owned a rather more exclusive car – a 1972 Rolls Royce Silver Cloud Convertible II – having developed a taste for the limousine during her marriage (from 1966-1969) to the German playboy billionaire Gunter Sachs.

Le Mépris
Brigitte Bardot in (right), and alongside (left), the Alfa Romeo of Jack Palance in *Le Mépris* (*Contempt* in the American market) by Jean-Luc Godard, released in 1963.

A fragment of Bardot automotive trivia not to be omitted is that she was a friend of Jean Charles, an importer of American cars in Paris. And it is through this connection that Bardot is seen advertising an AMC Pacer. In a totally kitsch image, she is pictured sitting on the bonnet of a strange-looking American hatchback that resembled a giant Renault 5. In her films, we also see her driving a modest Citroën 2CV in *Please, Not Now!* in 1961, and a Chevrolet Corvette in *The Bear and The Doll* in 1970. However, in what is without doubt the best film of her career (*Le Mépris*, or *Contempt* in the American market) directed by Jean-Luc Godard in 1963, Bardot (playing Camille Javal) gets a ride in the red 1962 Alfa Romeo 2600 Spider owned by Jeremy Prokosch, the millionaire playboy film producer played by Jack Palance. The car comes to represent both power and money, and after getting a lift from Palance, Camille's relationship with husband Paul Javal (Michel Piccoli) begins to unravel and contempt sets in. She leaves Paul, and heads for Rome with Prokosch in the Alfa, (with the memorable line: 'Get in your Alfa, Romeo ...'), but ultimately, towards a tragic end.

JEAN-LUC GODARD
ALFA-MALE

Explosive
In *Pierrot le Fou* (above, 1965), Godard incinerated a Peugeot 404, and in *Weekend* (1967) he smashed up a dozen cars, including his own Alfa Romeo.

Jean-Luc Godard, one of the giants of French New Wave cinema, was a lover of cars in general (and of Alfa Romeo in particular) and there is an automotive strand running through many of his films made during the 1960s. His first full-length feature, *Breathless* (1960), is the story of a car thief. Michel Poiccard, (Jean-Paul Belmondo), is seen stealing a 1955 Ford Thunderbird, a 1954 Cadillac convertible, and a 1956 Oldsmobile 88 – displaying Godard's taste for American cars, also evident in *Le Petit Soldat* in 1963. Godard, of course, was not the only French director of his time to enjoy the appearance of fine cars in his films. In Louis Malle's 1958 film

Lift To The Scaffold, Maurice Ronet drives a 1952 Chevrolet Deluxe, while a gull-wing Mercedes 300 SL has a key role in the plot. In *Trapped by Fear* in 1960 by Jacques Dupont, Belmondo plays the part of a photojournalist, driving an Austin-Healey 100-4 Roadster. All this led to some critics of the New Wave movement to dismiss the films as about little more than young layabouts driving sports cars. None of this discouraged Godard, who made the Alfa Romeo 2600 Spider one of the central characters in *Le Mépris* (see the previous article). Despite the accident that destroys this Alfa at the end of that film, the car reappears in *Pierrot le Fou* two years later. Anna Karina, who

---

LE MÉPRIS (1963)
Alfa Romeo 2600 Spider

PIERROT LE FOU (1965)
Alfa Romeo Giulietta 1600

WEEKEND (1967)
Alfa Romeo 2600 Sprint

plays Marianne Renoir, drives an Alfa Romeo Giulietta 1600, this time in blue. Jean-Luc Godard himself drove an Alfa Romeo, a luxurious dark blue 2600 coupé, but around the time of making *La Chinoise* (1967) and *Weekend* (the same year) his left-wing convictions came more strongly to the fore, and his relationship with cars visibly altered. In *Weekend*, he portrays a Parisian couple (played by Mireille Darc and Jean Yanne) driving a chic 1960 Facel Vega Facellia cabriolet – until they become stuck in the mother of all traffic jams. This film sets out to denounce the culture of cars, and ends with a

pile-up in which Godard chooses to sacrifice his very own car: his Alfa ends up in the mess of twisted metal. Following that, he got around on a motorbike until 1971, when he was victim of a serious road accident (he was actually run over by a bus) during the filming of *All's Well*. Godard was in a coma for a week, and then had to undergo three years of physio. Not surprisingly, cars, as well as motorbikes, featured a lot less prominently in his films after this.

Pierrot le Fou
Jean-Paul Belmondo, driving an Autobianchi Primula, leans across to kiss Anna Karina in her Alfa Romeo Giulietta Spider 1600 in *Pierrot le Fou* (1965). The film was seen as a precursor to the modern day road movie.

'DON'T USE THE BRAKES. CARS ARE MADE TO GO, NOT TO STOP!'
JEAN-PAUL BELMONDO IN *BREATHLESS* BY JEAN-LUC GODARD (1960).

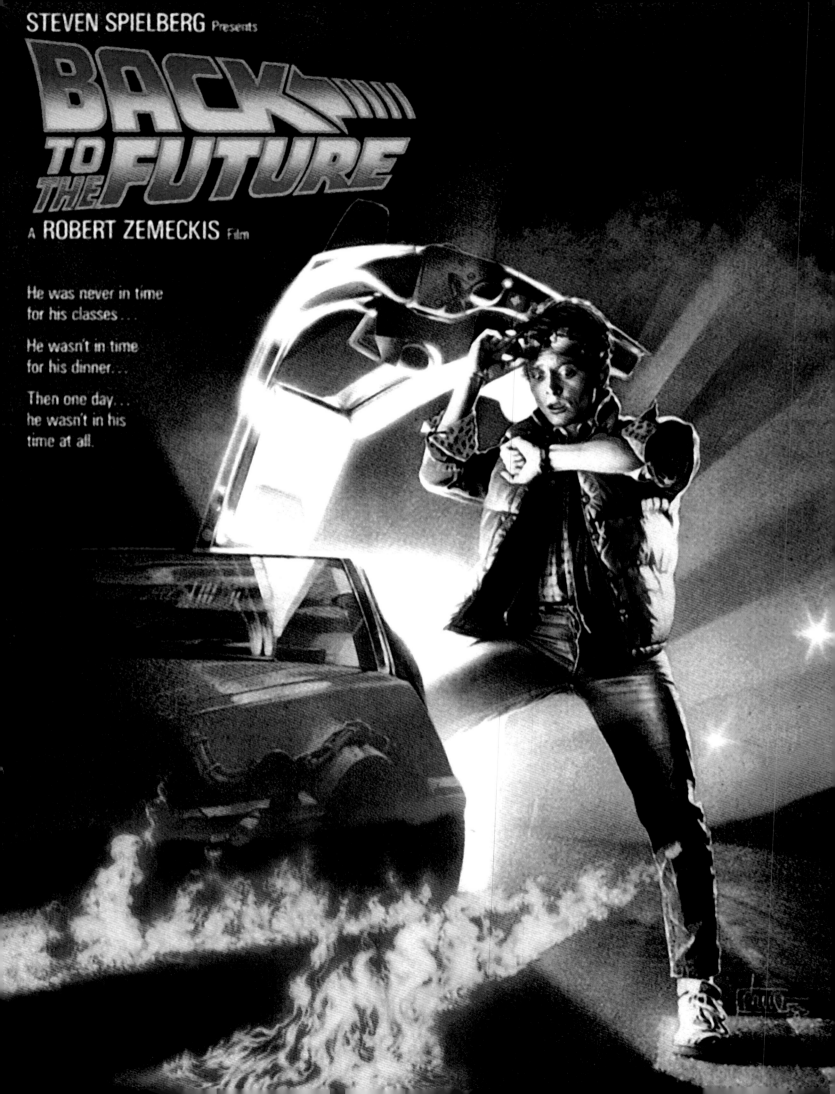

Back To The Future 2
Michael J Fox takes his flying
DeLorean forward to the future
in *Back To The Future 2* (1989),
and brings back a self-drying
jacket and some self-tying
trainers.

MICHAEL J. FOX
& DELOREAN

DMC-12 1983

'MARTY MCFLY: ARE YOU TELLING ME THAT
YOU BUILT A TIME MACHINE ... OUT OF A DELOREAN?
DR EMMETT BROWN: THE WAY I SEE IT, IF YOU'RE
GONNA BUILD A TIME MACHINE INTO A CAR,
WHY NOT DO IT WITH SOME STYLE?'

BACK TO THE FUTURE

Robert Zemeckis's decision to use a DeLorean DMC-12 as the time machine in *Back To The Future* propelled the car to instant international fame. In the film, the car has been seriously customized by time travel inventor Doc Brown (Christopher Lloyd), allowing Marty McFly (Michael J Fox) to make a return trip between the 1980s and the 1950s. Initially, Zemeckis and writer Bob Gale had thought of building the time machine not inside a customized car, but inside a full-size American fridge. But they quickly saw

the risk that small kids might try to copy the idea. So the fridge idea was dropped, and instead, the role of time machine was given to this dramatic, exclusive and also rather paradoxical car. The DMC itself was the brainchild of John Z DeLorean, who had been the youngest vice-president at General Motors during the 1960s, and who went on to gain wealth, celebrity and connections as a result of his success. While at GM, he pioneered the idea of product placement in films, of which the presence of his own DMC-12 in *Back To The Future* was a crowning achievement. He resigned from the carmaker to start his own sports car company in 1973, with funding from showbiz friends that included Sammy Davis Jr and Johnny Carson. His idea: to launch a sports coupé that would be unbreakable. He opened a factory in Northern Ireland to benefit from generous government subsidies in what was then an area

Back to the future
Doc (Christopher Lloyd)
demonstrates the control panel
of the DeLorean DMC-12 time
machine with Marty McFly
(Michael J. Fox)

of industrial decline. The dramatic-looking gullwing car was launched in 1981, helped along by British government subsidies, which were shortly afterwards withdrawn by prime minister Margaret Thatcher when he was arrested for trafficking cocaine, the result of a sting operation by the FBI.

In fact, the charges were later dropped when DeLorean was able to prove that the agents incited him to participate in their drugs trafficking operation. Despite the success of *Back To The Future* and its two sequels in 1989 and 1990, it was already too late to save DeLorean's troubled car company. When the first episode came out, in 1985, the factory was already closing down, having built only 9,200 DMC models in total – enough, though, for the car to become a legend. Michael J Fox became an instant star at the age of just 24, and went on to act in a series of comedies (*Teen Wolf*, *Doc Hollywood* ...) before hitting his stride with the series *Spin City*. Despite a diagnosis of early-onset Parkinson's disease at the age of just 30, Fox has continued his acting career, most recently as Louis Canning in American TV drama *The Good Wife*. Nonetheless, the combination of the young Michael J Fox and this strange gull-wing car remains an enduring image in cinematic history.

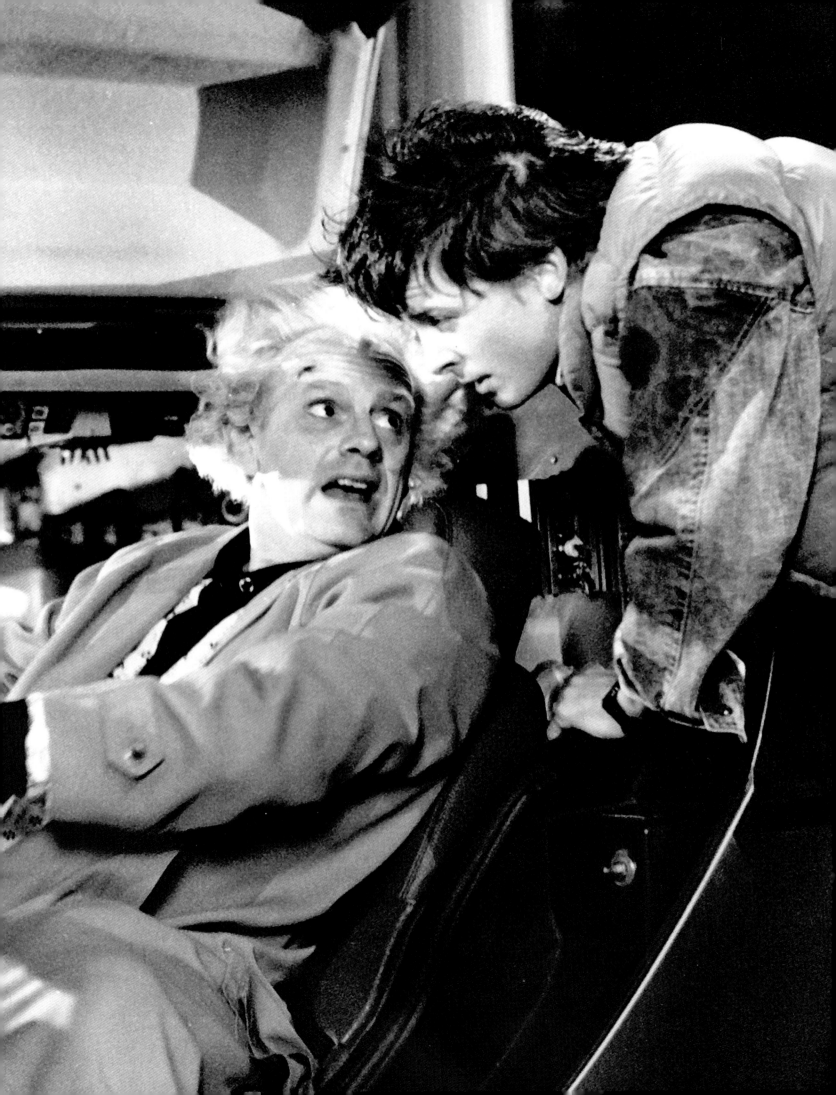

DELOREAN
1983 DMC-12

ENGINE
Configuration **6-cylinder, V6**
Capacity **2851 cc**
Fuel **Petrol**
Layout **Rear engine, longitudinal**

TRANSMISSION
Gearbox **5-speed, manual**
Drive type **Rear wheel drive**

DIMENSIONS
Length **4.21 m** / Width **1.85 m**
Height **1.14 m**
Weight **1230 kg**

PERFORMANCE
Power **130 bhp**
Maximum speed **125 mph**

① Rust-free

The bodywork of the DMC-12 is in stainless steel, which gives it the unique silver hue. Styling was by Italian designer Giugiaro (who created the look for the Lotus Esprit and the VW Golf).

② Plenty of spares

In 1997, the DeLorean Motor Company of Texas bought some of the tooling and the millions of parts that had been made to manufacture the planned 10,000 DMCs each year. Thanks to this, most of the 9,200 or so DeLoreans that were built are still running.

③ Want one?

You can even buy a brand new DeLorean, completely rebuilt, largely from the Texas company's stock of spare parts. It comes with a more powerful 300 bhp V6 engine – and there is also an electric version.

④ A serviceable engine

The initial idea was to use a rotary engine, but this looked to be too expensive to run, and too complex for the carmaker to create from scratch. The DMC-12 instead used a new V6 Peugeot-Volvo-Renault engine. It was only good for about 130 bhp, but was familiar enough so that any mechanic across Europe could service it.

BARRY NEWMAN
& DODGE
CHALLENGER

The driver is known only as Kowalski, and he is travelling the freeways of the western United States at breakneck speed, the police in hot pursuit. He stops at a bar to pick up some amphetamines, and meets a young woman, totally naked, riding a motorcycle, who wants to make love ... But let's re-wind for a moment. Richard Sarafian's *Vanishing Point* in 1971 is the archetypical road movie. The star is not the relatively unknown (at the time) Barry Newman, but the car that he is driving: a Dodge Challenger R/T, which is the 'large' Dodge sports model, compared with the more agile Charger. There is a similar story in Monte Hellman's cult drama *Two Lane Blacktop*, released the same year. Two drivers, whose names are never revealed, travel from town to town taking part in illegal drag racing. The star in this film is the matt grey Chevrolet Bel Air 55. Paradoxically, the very first film in the new road movie genre, two years earlier, did not use cars, but motorcycles. In 1969, two hippies travel across America on their Harley Davidson choppers – towards a tragic end. Dennis Hopper's *Easy Rider* is seen as the manifesto of a new Hollywood that explores a new freedom both of living life – and of making films. It went on to influence a large number of films involving cars, with their privileged place at the heart of the American imagination. These road movies are in a way a modern-day version of the Western, without native Americans or the settlers from the East, but often retaining the idea of the lone hero versus the cavalry: the individual versus the system, but at the wheel of a car, and against the backdrop of the counter-culture of the 1970s. Kowalski, in *Vanishing Point*, is the original cowboy, but with added backstory (he is a Vietnam vet, and a disillusioned ex-cop and a drug user). Neither *Vanishing Point* nor *Two Lane Blacktop* were instant box-office successes, but gained cult status as time went on, particularly with European audiences. And they went on to inspire dozens of other films, including *Dirty Mary, Crazy Larry* (1974) which was a big-budget road movie starring Peter Fonda, who had appeared in *Easy Rider* as Captain America.

THE ROAD MOVIE
BOX OFFICE WINNERS

You can see early aspects of the road movie as far back as John Ford's *The Grapes of Wrath* in 1940, or Arthur Penn's *Bonnie and Clyde* in 1967, or even *Pierrot le Fou* by Jean-Luc Godard in 1965. But the genre is more directly related to the B-movies of Roger Corman, such as *The Fast and the Furious* in 1955, (which lent its name to the current billion-dollar movie franchise). Also influential were some of Russ Meyer's films, such as *Faster, Pussycat! Kill! Kill!* in 1965, with his trio of hell-raising go-go dancers driving European sports cars (Porsche 356, MGA, Triumph TR3). Films like *Two Lane Blacktop* and *Vanishing Point* went on to be followed by much more popular riffs on

similar themes. Burt Reynolds became a legend in the USA thanks to *Smokey and the Bandit*. Driving a black 1977 Pontiac Trans Am decorated with an eagle painted in gold across the bonnet, in one scene he gives way to a truck loaded with contraband beer, with dozens of police cars in pursuit. On TV, *The Dukes of Hazzard* took up the same formula: a fast car (a 1969 Dodge Charger), a pretty girl (Daisy Duke, played by Catherine Bach), contraband, and epic car chases with the law enforcers, all with a Southern States twang and lashings of kitsch.

The road movie, however, could also take a very different route. In Terrence Malick's 1973 crime movie *Badlands*, the film takes on a contemplative

aspect, and features the surrounding habitat just as much as the 1959 Cadillac of Martin Sheen and Sissy Spacek.

Meanwhile, in Steven Spielberg's first film, *Duel* in 1971, he creates a road movie where the main character is an ordinary American in an ordinary car (a 1971 Plymouth Valiant), being pursued by a crazed truck driver. The following year, he pushed this further in *The Sugarland Express*, which portrays a camper van being pursued – slowly – by police cars, because the driver of the van has taken a police officer hostage.

European directors making films in the USA have often shown a tendency to make a different kind of road movie, using the genre to film images

VANISHING POINT (1971)
Dodge Challenger

TWO LANE BLACKTOP (1971)
Chevrolet Bel Air 1955

BADLANDS (1973)
Cadillac 1959

of their own idea of a mythical America: the beautiful cars, the desert, the motels, and the gas stations in the middle of nowhere. Michelangelo Antonioni approached this in *Zabriskie Point* in 1970, as did Wim Wenders with *Paris, Texas* in 1984. The road movie genre enjoyed something of a revival in the 1990s, but this time the films added an additional layer of references to American mythology, past and present.

Among Quentin Tarantino's early writing credits there are two good example of this. *True Romance*, with Patricia Arquette and Christian Slater, and *Natural Born Killers* with Juliette Lewis and Woody Harrelson: both are essentially road movies featuring vintage drop-top cars driven across the US by homicidal couples. The same goes for *Wild at Heart* in 1990 by David Lynch, with Laura Dern and Nicolas Cage,

or, the following year, *Thelma and Louise* by Ridley Scott, with Susan Sarandon and Geena Davis. Quentin Tarantino himself wrapped up this revival with *Death Proof* in 2007, a feminist and stylized version of the road movie, in which we see once more the white Dodge Challenger of Kowalski (from *Vanishing Point*) and an impressive Ford Mustang Mach 1 that Tarantino continued to use as his own personal car.

Thelma and Louise
A 1966 Ford Thunderbird cabriolet pursued by massed police cruisers in the desert: in 1991, Ridley Scott made a road movie about women.

SMOKEY AND THE BANDIT (1977)
Pontiac Trans Am 1977

THE DUKES OF HAZZARD (1977)
Dodge Charger 1969

DEATH PROOF (2007)
Ford Mustang Mach 1

Wild At Heart
Nicolas Cage and Laura Dern in their 1965 Ford Thunderbird cabriolet. David Lynch's *Wild at Heart* won the Palme d'Or at Cannes in 1990, and started a new wave of road movies during the 1990s.

JEFF BRIDGES

When they tried to buy him,
he refused.

When they tried to bully him,
he resisted.

When they tried to break him,
he became
an American legend.

The true story of
Preston Tucker.

TUCKER

JEFF BRIDGES
& TUCKER
1948 TORPEDO SEDAN

'AW, WHAT'S THE DIFFERENCE - FIFTY CARS OR FIFTY MILLION. THAT'S ONLY MACHINERY! IT'S THE IDEA THAT COUNTS, ABE ... THE DREAM ...'

JEFF BRIDGES IN *TUCKER*

In 1948, Preston Tucker launched a car that suddenly made every other American car look old-fashioned. Aerodynamic and very fast (around 120 mph), the Tucker 48 was equipped with an engine adapted from a helicopter, independent suspension front and rear, and it even had seat belts. But after building just 51 units of this revolutionary car, Preston Tucker had to throw in the towel, his project brought down by the Detroit establishment (Ford, General Motors, and Chrysler). That, at least, is the thesis of Francis Ford Coppola's 1988 film *Tucker: The Man and His Dream*, starring Jeff Bridges in the lead role. Coppola himself was a fan of fine cars, and owned the same classic Mercedes 600 limousine used by world leaders in previous decades including President Tito and Chairman Mao. And just like his friend George Lucas, who produced the film, he owned Tuckers, with Coppola in fact owning *two* of the 51 Tuckers ever produced. Coppola saw in the story of this independently minded carmaker a metaphor for his own experience in the film industry. He had founded the American studio Zoetrope with the aim of getting on equal terms with the Hollywood majors, but the project was ruinously expensive, and he managed only to produce three or four films each year.

Detroit
In *Tucker* (1988), Francis
Ford Coppola shows every
stage in the design of a car
during the golden age of
the US auto industry.

Jeff Bridges, the future *Big Lebowski*, creates
a Tucker who is a family man who loves fast cars
and eats his steak rare. He is above all straight-
talking businessman, calling to mind George
Bailey in Frank Capra's *It's A Wonderful Life*
(1947). He faces constant hostility from the
banks, which force him to hire a director who
comes straight from one of Tucker's rival
carmakers in Detroit. In one memorable and
chilling scene, the director tells Tucker he should
not fit seat belts to his cars, as this could make
customers believe the car is *not safe* if it needs
this kind of equipment. The film also shows the
gigantic post-war car factories, and all the stages
of the conception and creation of a new model. In
the final scene, when Tucker is reminded by his
colleague Abe Karatz that the factory only
managed to make 51 cars before shutting down,
Tucker replies: 'Aw, what's the difference - fifty or
fifty million. That's only machinery! It's the idea
that counts, Abe ... The dream ...' Amazingly, of
the 51 Tucker cars that were made, 49 are still
driving today: proof, perhaps, that Tucker's
dream was not far from becoming reality.

TUCKER
1948 TORPEDO SEDAN

ENGINE
Configuration **6-cylinder, horizontally opposed (H-6)**
Capacity **5473 cc**
Fuel **Petrol**
Layout **Rear engine, longitudinal**

TRANSMISSION
Gearbox **4-speed, manual, and 'Tuckermatic' CVT automatic**
Drive type **Rear wheel drive**

DIMENSIONS
Length **5.56 m** / Width **2.00 m**
Height **1.52 m**
Weight **1921 kg**

PERFORMANCE
Power **166 bhp**
Maximum speed **120 mph**

① Rear engine

The Tucker is one of the rare large sedans with a rear-mounted engine – just like the Czech Tatra, designed before the Second World War, and which remained the most interesting car from the Eastern Bloc right through to the fall of the Berlin Wall.

② Aero design

The styling of the Tucker draws heavily on aviation design of the period, which also assured class-leading aerodynamics. In 1950, Studebaker cars returned to this principle, quickly followed by America's big three carmakers for the rest of the decade.

③ Directional headlights

The Tucker is equipped with a third headlight in the middle of the grille, which turns in line with the steering of the wheels to provide better lighting on bends. Citroën used this idea on its DS, but worked with classic, lateral headlights.

COLUMBIA PICTURES presents

ROBERT DE NIRO

TAXI DRIVER

A BILL/PHILLIPS Production of a MARTIN SCORSESE Film

ROBERT DE NIRO
& CHECKER

MARATHON 1975

'... YOU TALKIN' TO ME ? THEN WHO THE HELL
ELSE ARE YOU TALKIN' TO ? YOU TALKIN' TO ME ?
WELL I'M THE ONLY ONE HERE. WHO THE F***
DO YOU THINK YOU'RE TALKING TO ?'

TRAVIS BICKLE IN *TAXI DRIVER*

Travis Bickle (Robert De Niro) is a taxi driver, working nights on the streets of Manhattan. A Vietnam veteran, he patrols the violent and broken New York of the 1970s. He gets involved with Betsy (Cybill Shepherd), an elegant lawyer that he sees some evenings, and dreams of becoming the saviour of Iris (Jodie Foster), an under-age prostitute who he believes wants to get off the streets. Violent and tortured, Travis sees himself as a vigilante: he wants to fight an exploding level of criminality in the city, and attack the robbers, drug dealers and pimps. His is shut inside his taxi, just as he feels trapped within the city and its madness.

When you think about it, a taxi is very much the opposite of a car. If you have a car, you have the power to drive wherever you want, simply on a whim. The taxi, by contrast, just drives around, and around. The car belongs to an individual. But the taxi belongs to everyone. In some films, such as Luc Besson's series *Taxi,* the taxi driver becomes a comedy figure. But in this film, he is the symptom of a city gone mad, of an era where people have lost their bearings. Travis's car is a Checker, the iconic New York City cab that was built from 1960 to 1982. It was popular with the city's drivers, and it was not uncommon still to see its characteristic silhouette even at the start of the 21st Century. As a symbol of a triumphant and successful America at the start of the 1960s, the Checker of *Taxi Driver*, released in 1976, represents the values that slowly faded out of American cities after the first oil crisis.

Travis
Following his role in *The Godfather: Part II*, the role of Travis Bickle made Robert De Niro a global star. And Scorsese's film won the Palme d'Or at the Cannes Film Festival in 1976.

Four years later, President Ronald Reagan, the ex-Hollywood actor from a golden age would be elected with the slogan: 'America is back.' But in New York, despite the new prosperity of the 1980s, it took the arrival of mayor Rudolph Giuliani, before the city started to take on a semblance of order with his 'zero tolerance' policies of which Travis Bickle would most certainly have approved. When De Niro was filming *Taxi Driver*, he had just appeared in Francis Ford Coppola's *The Godfather: Part II* which won him an Oscar for best supporting actor. *Taxi Driver* went on to receive the Palme d'Or at Cannes, and De Niro was to make a total of seven films with Martin Scorsese, including *Raging Bull* in 1980, which won him an Oscar for Best Actor.

De Niro's monologue in front of his rear-view mirror: 'You talkin' to me?' became a cult movie moment, and this dark and tortured film became a blockbuster success. Whether as a mafioso, boxer, or taxi driver, De Niro portrayed as never before the life of the city of New York, in all its excess and darkness.

PLEASE
DO NOT SLAM
DOOR

65¢ 1ST 1/6 MILE

TAXI BLUES

The Fifth Element (1997)
In the future, according to Luc Besson, taxis will fly – but Yellow Cabs will continue to be yellow.

In most classic American films, taxi drivers will count themselves lucky to get an appearance in just one shot, usually of the back of their head as they take the fare at the end of the ride. More likely though, the driver will not appear at all, and we will just see the yellow door open and a character step in, or climb out. But, in the 1970s, a new Hollywood was starting to change all the old rules. In *Taxi Driver* (1975), Scorsese put De Niro at the wheel of a Checker cab and opened up a whole new perspective on the city. In 1990, Russian director Pavel Lounguine took a similar approach with *Taxi Blues*. The tough-guy driver of an ancient 1973 Gaz Volga becomes friends with a dissident saxophone player, and together they explore a Moscow that seems on the verge of collapse. The

following year, Jim Jarmusch made a film about five taxi drivers (including Winona Ryder and Roberto Benigni) and their five clients (Gena Rowlands and Béatrice Dalle among them) in five cities across the world on the same evening, in his 1991 feature *Night on Earth*. More recently, in 2015, Jafar Panahi, banned from filming by the Iranian government, came up with an alternative: he put a camera into a taxi that he drove, and, from one journey to the next, conversed with real customers, as well as his friends, to make the film *Taxi Teheran*. But for less talk, and more action, how about a scenario where a young woman, on the run from her pursuers, happens to fall into a flying taxi being driven by Bruce Willis? This is exactly what happens in Luc Besson's *The Fifth Element* (1997). The following year saw

TAXI DRIVER (1976)
Checker Marathon 1975

TAXI BLUES (1990)
Gaz Volga 1973

TAXI (1998)
Peugeot 406

the release of Besson's *Taxi*, where a detective who can't drive teams up with an extremely fast taxi driver (Samy Naceri) in a souped-up Peugeot 406 taxi to chase down the bad guys. Following this, Besson created *The Transporter*, starring Jason Statham, and running from 2002 to 2008, in which Statham, in black Audi and matching black suit, is a tough-guy courier driver for criminal clients. Another director and producer who saw in the humble taxi the potential star of an action movie is Michael Mann. In *Collateral* in 2004, Michael Mann casts Jamie Foxx as a chauffeur who picks up an anxious client (Tom Cruise) at Los Angeles airport. Cruise courteously requests the driver to take him from one address to another, to a series of 'meetings'. And eventually, the truth dawns on the driver: the customer is a contract killer engaged in a series of murders. Suddenly, we have a new perspective: the taxi is not just driving through a violent city – it is driving that very violence right into the city.

Night on Earth
Winona Ryder, Los Angeles cab driver in *Night on Earth* (1991) by Jim Jarmusch.

BATMAN
& BATMOBILE

Batman
Michael Keaton in Batman costume in the 1989 *Batman* film by Tim Burton. Keaton also gets to drive the incredible turbine-powered Batmobile.

Superman can fly. Spiderman jumps from building to building, thanks to his web. And the X-Men have their plane, a Lockheed SR-71 Blackbird big enough for the whole lot of them. As for Batman, well, in truth he is a bit lacking in superpowers, with his wings and cables operating, at best, as a kind of elevator. So right from the start, if he were going to hunt down crime in the suburbs of Gotham City, he would have to get himself a car. In the original comic strips, this happened in 1939, a year after the character was launched, and the car he used was a red coupé. In 1941, the car became black, and was given a grille motif in the form of a menacing bat head, and a distinctive wing-shaped tailfin on the same theme. And the rest, in terms of Batmobiles, is history. As luck would have it, Batman's alter ego, Bruce Wayne, is a billionaire, and has bottomless funds to upgrade his cars and the incredible gadgets they contain: rockets, Bat Signal, radar, a 1950s-era computer, a crime predicting system, and so on. Notable too in this armoury are the radioactive tyres from 1940, which from today's perspective are slightly worrying. There was a change of style in the 1960s, with a futuristic coupé equipped with plexiglass bubble-like canopies which went on to inspire the Batmobile of the TV series in 1966.

The Dark Knight
In Christopher Nolan's trilogy (2005-2012) Christian Bale, as Bruce Wayne, drives a Lamborghini Murcielago cabriolet. His other car is the Tumbler.

To bring the car into being, the producers called on the services of George Barris, a pioneer of customized cars, and famous for his 'chopped' Mercury 49 with lowered suspension. For the Batmobile, Barris was inspired by the Lincoln Futura, a 1956 concept car made with the Italian coachbuilder Ghia. Painted in black, with the addition of tailfins and red stripes, this Batmobile became a star of the miniatures available in the Hot Wheels series. In 1989, Tim Burton pushed the envelope even further in the first *Batman* movie. He gave Michael Keaton a neo-classical sports version of the Batmobile, reminiscent of the coupés from the 1930s. The motor was replaced by an enormous turbine, though quite how it worked was never revealed.

In *Batman Begins* in 2005, the first in Christopher Nolan's *Dark Knight* trilogy, Bruce Wayne (Christian Bale), as well as being a billionaire, is an arms dealer too. So Bale is thus driving the Tumbler – a vehicle that resembles a kind of postmodern and extremely fast assault vehicle, jaw-dropping if not exactly seductive, and in stark contrast to the Lamborghini Murcielago that he drives when he wants to be taken for an idle and extremely rich playboy. Most recently, in Zack Snyders's *Batman v Superman: Dawn of Justice* in 2016, Ben Affleck as Bruce Wayne gets an even more incredible version of this racing tank than his predecessor. Nonetheless, he also has a soft spot for the Aston Martin DB2 MkIII of 1957 that he uses to go to one of his charity fund-raisers. So as well as being a billionaire and a playboy, and a superhero, he is a philanthropist. Lucky man.

BATMOBILE
TUMBLER

ENGINE
Configuration **8-cylinder, V8**
Capacity **5 733 cc**
Fuel **Petrol**
Layout **Mid-engine, transverse**

TRANSMISSION
Gearbox **Unknown**
Drive type **4-wheel drive**

DIMENSIONS
Length **4.57 m** / Width **2.84 m**
Height **1.50 m**
Weight **2300 kg**

PERFORMANCE
Power **500 bhp**
Maximum speed **160 mph**

① Stealth style

The design of the Batmobile Tumbler is inspired by that of stealth aircraft such as the Lockheed Nighthawk. It is also a style evident on the Lamborghini that Batman drives in his private life, though in a somewhat restrained version.

② Call it Tumbler

The Tumbler is resolutely modern, with the front wheels inverted, inspired by military vehicle design, and a far cry from the rather baroque and fancy Batmobiles of the past. In fact, it is never referred to as a 'Batmobile' in any of the three films in which it appears.

③ Gadgets galore

Among the many features the Tumbler has at its disposal, there are mini-jet engines that will allow the whole vehicle to jump two metres. Its extensive weaponry includes a rocket launcher and a machine gun mounted in a retractable tower.

INDEX CARS

STARS

FILMS & SERIES

CREDITS

Cover (above) : © John Dominis/The LIFE Picture Collection/Getty Images; (below) : © James Vaughan

Page 6 : © John Kobal Foundation/Getty Images; pages 12, 206 : © Movie Poster Image Art/Getty Images; page 15 : © Silver Screen Collection/Getty Images; page 16 : © AKG-images/Album/Solar/Cinema Center; pages 18, 64, 144 : © Phil Talbot/Alamy Stock Photos/Hemis.fr; page 20 : © Collection CSFF/Bridgeman Images; page 22 : © Warner Bros/The Kobal Collection/AFP; pages 24, 146, 149 : © Photos 12.com – Collection Cinéma/AFP; pages 25, 152 : © Archives du 7e Art/Photo12/AFP; page 26 : © Monitoring Picture Library/Alamy Stock Photos/Hemis.fr; pages 28, 48, 53, 83, 86, 200 : © Rue des Archives/BCA; pages 29, 100 : © Keystone France; pages 31, 77, 210 : © Kobal/The Picture Desk/AFP; page 32 : © Rainer W. Schlegelmilch/Getty Images; pages 34 (BL), 34 (BM), 34 (BR), 35 (BL), 35 (BM), 35 (BR), 47, 52 (BL), 52 (BM), 54 (BR), 79 (BL), 79 (BM), 79 (BR), 96 (BL), 96 (BM), 96 (BR), 97 (BL) 97 (BM), 97 (BR), 104, 124 (BL), 124 (BM), 124 (BR), 125 (BL), 125 (BM), 125 (BR) 130 (BL), 130 (BM), 130 (BR), 150, 166 (BL), 166 (BM), 166 (BR), 167 (BL), 167(BM), 167 (BR), 186 (BL), 186 (BM), 186 (BR), 196 (BL), 196 (BM), 196 (BR), 197 (BL), 197 (BM), 197 (BR), 210 (BL), 210 (BM), 210 (BR) : © DR; page 35 (above) : © Pierre Vauthey/Sygma/Corbis; pages 38, 152 : © Rue des Archives/Everett; page 41 : © Bridgeman Images; page 42 : © Keith Hamshere/Kobal/The Picture Desk/AFP; page 44 : © ED/RM/Camerapress/Gamma-Rapho; page 51 : © Camerapress/Gamma-Rapho; page 54 : © Denis Cameron/Pix Inc./The LIFE Picture Collection/Getty Images; page 57 : © Botti/Stills/Gamma; page 58 : © Chestnot/Getty Images; page 60: © Archives du 7e art/Riama Film/AFP; page 63 : © Riama Film/Gray-Film/Pathé Co/Collection Christophel/AFP; pages 68, 71: © Kennedy Miller Productions/Village Roadshow Pictures/The Kobal Collection/AFP; page 69 : © API/Gamma; page 72 : © Ruaridh Connellan/Barcroft Cars/Abacapress.com; pages 74, 76 : © Universal/The Kobal Collection/AFP; pages 78, 102, 103, 106, 118, 124 (above gauche), 136, 137 : © Corbis; page 79 (above): © AKG-images/Album/Warner Bros Pictures/Syncopy; pages 80, 189 : © Archives du 7e art/Universal Pictures/AFP; page 84 : © Relativity Media/Universal/The Kobal Collection/Aurimages; page 89 : © Bold Films/The Kobal Collection; page 90 : © akg-images/Album/Paramount; pages 91, 93 : Paramount/The Kobal Collection/Aurimages; page 94 : © Darryl Norenberg/The Enthusiast Network/Getty Images; page 97 (above) : © akg-images/Album/Warner Brothers; pages 108, 111 : © Frank Worth, Courtesy of Capital Art/Getty Images; page 112 : © Superstock/Rue des Archives; pages 114, 140 : © Rue des Archives/RDA; pages 115, 131 : © Archive Photos/Intermittent/Getty Images; page 117 : © MGM/The Kobal Collection/AFP; page 120 : © Reg Lancaster/Daily Express/Hulton Archive/Getty Images; page 122 : Jean-Louis Quequet/Gamma; page 125 (above) : © EPA/Georgios Kefalas/Corbis; page 126 : © David Seymour/Magnum Photos; pages 134, 170 : © Rue des Archives/Collection CSFF; page 138 : © Robert George/Magic Car Pics; page 143 : © PVDE / Bridgeman Images; page 148 : © AKG-images/Interfoto; page 155 : © NBC/NBCU Photo Bank via Getty Images; page 156 : © Martin/JTP/Photononstop; page 158 : © Lionsgate/Collection Christophel; page 160 : © Randy Holt/The Enthusiast Network/Getty Images; page 161 : LionsgateTelevision/Collection Christophel/AFP; page 164 : © The Ronald Grant Archive/Photononstop; page 165 : © Jean Baptiste Lacroix/WireImage/Getty Images; page 167 (above) : © 2011 Showtime Networks Inc/Collection Christophel; page 168 : © CBS/Getty Images; page 171 : © DR Ferret-Photographic; page 172 : © Richard Dredge/Magic Car Pics; page 176 : Warner Bros/The Kobal Collection/Aurimages; page 178 : © MagicCarPics archive; page 180 : © 2003 Getty Images; page 182 : © 2004 Getty Images; page 184 : © Rue des Archives/Collection CRFF; page 185 : © John Springer Collection/Corbis/Corbis via Getty Images; page 186 : © akg-images; page 187 : © akg-images/Album/Rome-Paris/Beauregard; page 188 : © Rue des Archives/RDA; page 191 : © Amblin/Universal/The Kobal Collection/AFP; page 192 : © culture-image GmbH/Alamy Stock Photo/Hemis.fr; page 194 : © 20th Century Fox/The Kobal Collection/AFP; page 197 (above) : © 2012 Getty Images; page 198 : © Acey Harper/Getty Images; pages 201, 211, 215 : © akg-images/Album; page 203 : Paramount/Getty Images; page 204 : © Copyright 2007 Corbis; page 207 : © akg-images/Album/Columbia Pictures; page 209 : © Columbia/The Kobal Collection/AFP; page 212, 216 : © Warner Bros/DC Comics/The Kobal Collection/AFP.